MW00777778

You Were Born to Heal

Hope and Transformation
from Divorce and Separation

Vance A. Taylor

You Were Born to Heal

Copyright © 2023 Vance Andrée Taylor
All Rights Reserved. Published 2023.

ISBN: 978-1-6653-0794-9 - Paperback
eISBN: 978-1-6653-0795-6 - eBook

This ISBN is the property of BookLogix for the express purpose of sales and distribution of this title. BookLogix is not responsible for the writing, editing, or design/appearance of this book. The content of this book is the property of the copyright holder only. BookLogix does not hold any ownership of the content of this book and is not liable in any way for the materials contained within. The views and opinions expressed in this book are the property of the Author/Copyright holder, and do not necessarily reflect those of BookLogix.

Library of Congress Control Number: 2023917365

Printed in the United States of America

Vance Andrée Taylor
P.O. Box 481316
Charlotte, North Carolina 28269
www.youwereborntoheal.com

Writing and publishing support
provided by The Write Image Consulting, LLC, and WriteYourLife.net

Book design by Emily Roberts, BeSpeak Designs
https://bespeakdesigns.com

The contents of this book are for educational purposes and nothing contained herein should be construed as life advice. The information provided in this book is not a complete analysis of every material fact for any life situation. Opinions expressed are subject to change without notice. Statements of fact cited have been obtained from sources considered reliable. No representation, however, is made as to the completeness or accuracy of any statement or data. This publication may include technical or other inaccuracies or typographical errors. Author assumes no responsibility for errors or omissions in this publication or other documents, which are referenced by or linked to this publication or the related website. Nothing contained herein is, in any way, a guarantee or assurance that following strategies outlined in this book will create success or security, and readers should understand that they are responsible for the actions they take or do not take as a result of reading this book.

What people are saying about Vance Andrée Taylor

"Vance A. Taylor is a phenomenal relationship coach who offers compassion and sound advice to those looking to have fulfilling and well-balanced personal lives. As someone who has lived through divorce and re-entered the world of dating and relationships, Vance is a great go-to source as a repeat panelist on our platforms bringing the male perspective. The audience always walks away with tangible advice to help them move forward. This life-changing book is indicative of Vance's desire to help others by sharing his personal journey from brokenness to healing. Congratulations!"

Kelli K. Fisher, Owner/Partner, The Matchmaking DUO
President, The Savvy Solo Parent

"Vance helped me look into myself and recommended ways to grow as an individual. I highly recommend his coaching to anyone looking to improve through self-awareness."
Sebastian G.

"Encouraging, thoughtful, motivating, non-judgmental, funny, and an all-around amazing coach and person. Vance has not only provided me useful insights, new tools, and fresh perspectives quickly, but has been a great help in finding strategies to navigate challenges in business, relationships, and life overall."
Ebony W.

"At the lowest point in my professional and personal life, when my mental and emotional state was in a tug of war, Vance came to the rescue and created balance. Not only did his techniques and emotional IQ intelligence offer comfort and much-needed guidance, but his communication style and his flexibility gave me an outlet to express myself and seek assistance at times I needed it the most. He was always present and responsive to my needs. His training in the areas I needed — career and relationship coaching — was top notch. As a result, my entire outlook on life and my relationships (personal and business) became more positive, and I am now present in all interactions."
Akilah S.

"Vance formulated a tailored recovery regimen for me that consisted of me doing self-introspection, self-accountability, and self-awareness of the conditions I considered adverse. Vance is awesome and his incredible regimen is designed to identify your weakness and assist you in mental strength conditioning in those areas. I am proof that it works. It is without hesitation nor mental reservation that I highly recommend his services." **LeNorah H.**

"I met Vance when I was emotionally broken from a recent breakup, and he made me feel more confident in my ability to recognize patterns and red flags that could lead to a failing relationship. One of the main things I took away from our coaching sessions was to ensure that my values are aligned."
Melanie B.

BONUS

Download your free copy of the Grow Through What You Go Through worksheet, designed to help you gain a better perspective of how to survive and thrive during and after your divorce.

Use it as a guide for healing and growth, and to bring joy and fulfillment into your life again.

www.youwereborntoheal.com/bonus

To my mom, my first love,
and my number one fan and supporter.

And to my son, VJ.
My love for you is unconditional.
Find your light and let it shine.
The fruit is in the seed.

Thanks for being one of my early readers Sadie! Your feedback was valuable, and helped to shape some of my message by giving me some additional things to think about. Enjoy the read! Continue to be an inspiration and beacon of hope for those who are dealing with divorce!

Vael. Tayl

Table of Contents

Introduction

It hurt like hell, but there wasn't much blood.

I was on my last exercise in a CrossFit competition and determined to finish strong. My heart was racing, my adrenaline pumping as I competed against the clock and other CrossFitters around me, which was probably why I didn't feel the initial pain. With thirty seconds left in the competition, I tightened my grip on the bar and did as many pull-ups as I could.

Despite being extremely tired and short of breath, I focused on not stopping until time ran out. I managed to get another ten pull-ups in before the clock ran down and I let go of the bar. But as soon as my feet touched the ground, I felt a sharp pain that nearly brought me to tears.

The inside of my hand felt like it was being stung by bees, and the burning sensation intensified by the second. I didn't realize it at the time, but the friction generated between the metal pull-up bar and the palm of my right hand was enough to rub off a layer of skin the size of a dime. Fortunately, that was the last exercise of the competition. Otherwise, I would've had to stop before it was over.

Despite the congratulatory remarks for pushing through the workout and comments about the overall competition itself, I could only think about how to keep my hand out of harm's way. The wider I opened it the more intense the pain became, so I kept my hand balled in a soft fist.

What took place in a matter of seconds on the pull-up bar ended up influencing certain areas of my life for days afterwards. I had to find ways to adapt in order to move forward. Handshakes became fist bumps. Routine activities, such as opening doors and brushing my teeth, required more thought and maneuvering than usual, not to mention more time. As a righty, I was forced to rely on my left hand more, which felt awkward. Things I once did without much thought or effort now required careful planning and execution.

I knew time would naturally do its part to heal the wound. However, I had to do my part as well. I had to aid time with that process and reduce the risk of reinjuring myself. Healing my wound would require special care and effort, especially in the beginning when it was most vulnerable to infection and re-injury.

I followed a routine that you're probably familiar with and have followed with your own injuries. I dabbed it with some alcohol (which burned), rubbed some ointment on it, and then covered it with a Band-Aid. I repeated this process for a few days, and I could tell it was beginning to heal when the alcohol no longer burned and a thin protective layer of skin formed over the wound. At that point, I no longer needed the alcohol, although I continued to put ointment on it to help reduce scarring and wore a Band-Aid to keep the new layer of skin from rubbing off.

Soon, a scab formed, relieving me of my ointment-and-bandage protective duties. After the scab came off, I was left with a small scar that has since faded to a point where I can no longer see it. With time and care, the wound healed itself, and I was finally able to get back to a life I knew before the injury. Only this time, I had more awareness of what to do to help prevent a similar injury.

What happened to my hand physically and the process it went through to heal can be compared to the experience you'll go through with your divorce, mentally and emotionally. For me, the journey was the same.

The "friction" leading up to the divorce, the initial pain and my sensitivity to it, how vulnerable I became as a result of the wounds, the nurturing needed to nurse them back to health and prevent further injury, the life adjustments I had to make to cope, the growth and lessons learned along the way—divorce impacted my life in multiple ways. Some of them took longer to heal from than others.

Getting to a place of healing wasn't easy, nor did it happen overnight. For more than a year, I wrestled with a range of negative emotions—anger, bitterness, confusion, and sadness, to name a few. Depending on the day, I might be angry and resentful in the morning and happy and at peace by the afternoon. My emotions were all over the place.

The experience changed me in ways I didn't expect. I began to shy away from social events out of fear of judgment and embarrassment. I sabotaged seemingly good relationships whenever I felt they were becoming too serious. My closest friends and family were married, so despite their best efforts to ease my pain, they couldn't relate to what I was going through. This led to countless days and nights of prayer and self-reflection, as well as periods of time when I acted out of character.

The more I focused on what I could control, the less of a negative impact the divorce had on me. I began to see and experience life differently because my thoughts and perspectives began to change. I took more responsibility for my joy and happiness and those things that were fulfilling, which led to growth and transformation. I followed a self-care routine that I continue to use a lot to this day.

It's natural for you to experience some form of pain — expressed as anger, bitterness, fear, embarrassment, resentment, or sadness — from your divorce. Those "emotional wounds," as I call them, are part of the experience, and they follow a healing process similar to the one I went through after my physical injury and my own divorce.

My experience is not unique. Millions of people from all walks of life have and will continue to experience divorce and the various challenges that come along with it. In addition to my own, I'll share some personal stories from clients of mine, whose names have been altered, to give you insight into what they experienced. A divorce can be one of the most confusing and trying periods of life. With it comes emotional pain and an uncertainty about the future. It can also include concerns about co-parenting and adjusting to being single again. It represents a loss, not just of the marriage, but also of dreams and commitments once shared. Families are broken apart, routines are disrupted, friendships are lost, finances are ruined. A divorce can cause a host of negative impacts in different areas of your life.

The hopes and dreams you once shared with your ex and the type of love you had for each other are gone. You go from spending time growing together to sleepless nights alone. From laughing and enjoying each other's company to crying and avoiding each other as much as possible.

It's not uncommon to socially withdraw because of what others may think or say. It's not unusual to jump into unhealthy relationships because of loneliness and lack of intimacy, to have your self-esteem and confidence shaken by questions and doubts, or to lose your desire to open up your heart again to another relationship. The impacts of a divorce can go wide and deep.

The good news is you were born to heal—not overnight, as you may wish, but naturally with time and an effective self-care routine. The amount of time it takes to heal and the degree to which you do so are heavily influenced by the quality of your self-care routine.

A routine that lacks introspection, patience, and a willingness to change or make certain adjustments within yourself will lead to partial healing or none at all. You're liable to carry some form of residual pain from the divorce into your next relationship and possibly repeat some of the same mistakes that led to your broken marriage.

You Were Born to Heal was written to help you do the opposite of that.

You'll learn how to manage the ups and downs of your emotions, engage in activities that aid in the healing process and deepen your sense of self, better prepare for intimate relationships as you begin meeting and dating people of long-term interest, and leverage what you're going through for growth and transformation.

This work will help boost your confidence and self-esteem while you make more informed decisions in life as a whole, not just in your relationships. With the right attitude and effort, you'll emerge from this experience a healthier and more aware person, mentally, emotionally, and spiritually.

Notice that I didn't mention anything about this process being easy. Through lived experience, I recognize and understand it won't be for most people. There are no detours on the road to recovery. You'll experience challenges and setbacks along the way, especially in the beginning. Recognize this as a natural part of the healing process. Have faith in it and give it time. Focus only on what you can control, and go with the flow of life from there.

Having been divorced for fifteen years now, I'm able to write this book from a more mature perspective, as a D.A.D. (Dater After Divorce). My journey has given me tools and insights that I use to help others heal and avoid some of the pitfalls that I fell into. Depending on where you are in your divorce journey, some exercises that I ask you to do may invoke certain emotional reactions that you're not ready to deal with yet, which is fine. This book was written with your current and future state in mind, so come back to them when you are ready. They serve a purpose.

Chapter 1.

The Past: How'd You Get Here?

Think about the past only in terms of how it relates to your present, which is where healing and transformation take place. After all, you can't change what happened. You can only learn from it and move forward. That's what you're here to do.

Every divorcee has a story. Perhaps you can relate to mine, which began long before I met my ex-wife. Although we both played a part in the marriage's demise, I believe my part had much more to do with a lack of self-awareness and with ego than it did with my wife. When I use the word "ego," I'm talking about my inability or unwillingness to see beyond myself in certain situations. This was the self-seeking part of me.

It wasn't until after my divorce was final, when I was on my transformational journey, that I took a hard look at what had happened to my marriage. I recommend you do the same on your journey. We'll go into this more a bit later.

Prior to that time, I blamed everything on my ex, turning a blind eye to my own transgressions. As far as I was concerned, she was the reason we were divorced. I had convinced myself of that and challenged anyone who said anything different. That was all based on a really big ego and a bit of shortsightedness on my part at the time. I only looked at negative situations that occurred throughout the course of our relationship—our dating life included—as the ultimate reason for the divorce. I examined everything that was or wasn't done from the time we met. However, I didn't take into consideration any prior relationships, romantic or otherwise, as a possible influence in our divorce.

When we first met, I didn't have a strong sense of what it took to maintain a healthy relationship or what I needed from a life partner. My relationship values, my boundaries, my ideal mental and spiritual characteristics, my love language — none of it was clearly defined. Up until my ex, I hadn't been able to make a lasting connection with anyone for longer than a couple years.

Back then, I placed more emphasis on superficial characteristics, like looks, than those that nourished my heart and soul. I often allowed what I saw to more heavily influence how I felt, instead of how I felt to heavily influence what I saw. As I would later discover, this is common for a lot of guys, especially at an early age. The foundation of what I thought a relationship should be lacked depth and understanding. As a result, I adapted to more of what my partners wanted and valued, some of which conflicted with who I was at my core.

To be fair, I was in my early twenties when the woman who would become my wife and I first met. I was young and still learning who I was as a person. And so was she. We were both operating within our level of consciousness at the time, most of which was based on our past experiences and conditioning. We were a product of our environments, and didn't know any different.

One of the things I failed to do prior to meeting my wife was to take the time necessary to understand why my previous relationships had ended and what changes I needed to make within to be a better partner in my next relationship. Instead, I boiled the majority of these break-ups down to a simple, safe, philosophical statement I had adopted over the years: "It wasn't meant to be."

To a certain extent, that was true. I'm a firm believer that everything happens for a reason and is purposeful in some way, not all of which I'll understand. Some things continue to happen because I haven't learned the lesson yet, and I keep repeating the same mistakes. At that time, I was guarded, which made it easier for me to detach emotionally and move on, using that statement as justification for the breakup instead of taking into consideration any possible lessons to be learned. Suppressing my feelings to avoid any pain became the default reaction. I had more of a fearful-avoidant attachment style back then, when it came to intimate relationships, which I'll talk more about later.

Had I done some self-reflecting back then, I'd like to think I would have uncovered certain patterns that were destructive to my relationships, such as the residual trust issues I carried into each one of them. I was afraid to fully open my heart up to someone. This lack of trust didn't develop because I had been cheated on or taken advantage of by any of my previous girlfriends. This issue stemmed from a broken relationship with my biological father, whose lies and false promises, which I endured as an adolescent, led to hurt and disappointment.

To avoid repeating that kind of emotional experience, I

put my guard up with him, and that guard never left its post. I conditioned myself at a young age not to believe anything he said. I still loved him and showed him respect the very few times we did talk or see each other, but I'd allow him to get only so close. I didn't want to be vulnerable, not realizing that being vulnerable is what's necessary to connect with someone on a deeper level in intimate relationships.

Little did I realize that this defense mechanism I created would have unintentional consequences in intimate relationships outside of my relationship with my dad. In some ways, I went into those relationships expecting lies and false promises. To avoid being hurt, I would keep my friends and girlfriends at an emotional distance, rarely allowing true intimacy a chance to evolve. Add to that some of my selfish desires and egotistical ways, and I had created a formula that wasn't conducive to a healthy relationship.

I share this story with you to underscore the importance of self-reflection. So much of who you are in romantic relationships is shaped by your upbringing and those critical relationships with parents, caregivers, siblings, other relatives, and influencers in your young life. Understanding your relationship history, not just the situations within your marriage that led to divorce, will give you more insight on changes you need to make for a different outcome moving forward.

Most people don't get married with divorce in mind. For various reasons, however, divorce happens to people from all walks of life. Maybe you were the victim of infidelity or abuse in a previous relationship, or your marriage lacked intimacy. You may have gotten caught up in the idea of being married, going into it for reasons that lacked substance. Maybe you didn't spend enough time getting to know your future spouse before saying, "I do," and you later discovered things about them that weren't a good fit or things that were difficult to deal with. Maybe your financial struggles became too much to bear, or the two of you just grew apart. The list of potential reasons for the demise of any relationship is both deep and wide.

I often ask people when discussing divorce: "Was the marriage doomed from the start, or did something happen during the marriage that caused it to end?" The responses I get vary, with a lot of them falling somewhere in between. Some felt pressure from those closest to them and married someone they were not compatible with to appease their loved ones. Others were deceived throughout the courtship, only to find a completely different person after their wedding vows. Still others married someone based on potential or false promises that never manifested, or they got married despite the internal warning bells or verbal warnings from family and friends.

Divorce doesn't happen overnight, it happens over time. Just like the constant friction against the pull-up bar weakened the skin on my palm and led to the wound, there are often a series of events that transpire during a marriage which chip away at its foundation. Those chips become cracks that grow deeper and longer over time. If the proper repairs aren't made, or they're made too late, the foundation of the marriage will eventually crumble. This is what leads to divorce.

For some people, a sequence of events prior to marriage contributes to the divorce. They bring unresolved issues from their own past relationships into the marriage, and those issues contribute to its demise. Self-reflection is an important part of the healing process after divorce, one I recommend as a part of your self-care routine.

Look at your relationship journey as a whole, not just within the context of your marriage, but also with previous partners. What was your relationship with them like? Understanding what happened in your previous relationships and the mistakes you made along the way will help you identify certain characteristics within yourself that may need to change. Find the lessons yet to be learned. They're at the core of your transformation process.

Through this process, you'll gain more insight into the choices you make, why you make them, and how those choices impact your relationships. You can leverage that awareness to help improve in other areas of your life as well, such as your interactions with friends and family members. You can then make different decisions that align you more with your goals, whether that's a healthier, more fulfilling relationship in the future or some other outcome you'd like to achieve.

If this is your first divorce, you are not alone. In fact, data from the U.S. Census Bureau shows that nearly half of all first-time marriages in the U.S. will end in divorce, with the average length of those marriages being eight years. Twenty percent of all marriages will end in divorce within the first five years, while 32% will end in divorce within the first ten years. When it comes to frequency, the first two years, otherwise known as the "honeymoon period," and years five to eight, have the highest divorce rates.[1]

In a June 2022 report by Divorce Strategies Group written by Denise French, about 70% of divorcees will end up remarrying, with the average length of time between marriages being 3.7 years. The divorce rate for second marriages is much higher, however, at around 67%, or every two out of three, which I found surprising.[2]

Those statistics represent a real need for divorcees looking to

---

1   Miles Mason, "Divorce Rates Statistics and Trends for 2022," Miles Mason Family Law Group, accessed June 24, 2023, https://memphisdivorce.com/tennessee-divorce-law/divorce-rates-statistics-and-trends-for-2022/#_edn23

2   Denise French, "Why Second Marriages Fail," Divorce Strategies Group, June 20, 2022, https://divorcestrategiesgroup.com/why-second-marriages-fail/

remarry one day to do the necessary work to heal and grow from the experience. I recommend that work include rediscovering who you are—your likes, dislikes and what brings you joy, happiness, and a sense of peace. Challenge old thought patterns and embrace new experiences. Begin to live the life you desire. As a result, you'll begin to generate a different kind of energy within that you'll project in your conversations and actions, and you'll align best with people you connect with beneath the surface.

My initial assumption was that second marriages would have a lower divorce rate than first marriages simply because of the lessons learned. If people decide to do it again, then I expected they'd go into a second marriage with more insight and awareness of who to align themselves with as a life partner and what it takes to make that marriage work. They would have an understanding of where they went right and wrong in their first marriage, I thought, so the second one should go the distance. But apparently that's not always the case. There are a number of reasons second marriages don't last, some of which are outside of our control. Much of what I see and hear from people who struggle in relationships after their divorce is that they don't give themselves enough time to heal from the wounds of their first marriage. They don't dedicate enough time for introspection or put the work in I mentioned earlier.

Some people hastily jump into another relationship because of their age, because they want kids, or because they're afraid of being alone. Others feel compelled because of pressure from family members or the need to conform to societal norms and fears of being ostracized. As a result, they ignore warning signs, set unrealistic expectations, fail to enforce boundaries, and overlook significant characteristics in their new partner. This leads them to connect with someone they're incompatible with, or they bounce from relationship to relationship with no connection at all.

That was the case with one of my clients, who I'll call Sarah. Sarah was in her early fifties and had been divorced for several years. She had involved herself in a series of dead-end relationships with men who took advantage of her strong desire to be in a committed relationship. She was getting older and was afraid of being alone forever, a fear that a lot of divorcees, and people in general, have. As a result, she compromised some of her values by having sex on the first date and always being accessible without the same in return. To find what she was really looking for, she needed to take some time away from dating to reflect on her relationship patterns.

After a divorce, moving forward in a healthy way requires some introspection. You're not the same person coming out of your marriage as you were going into it, so it's important that you spend some quality time reconnecting with yourself. The experience may have weakened your self-esteem and confidence or caused you to develop trust issues and biases, all of which can impact other areas of your life, and future relationships, in a negative way.

With self-reflection comes awareness, and that awareness opens the door for change. It can help you identify the reasons behind certain choices you make and why you react the way you do in various situations. Once you're conscious of what's happening, you can then elect to accept those choices and reactions as a part of who you are, or you can make changes to create a different outcome or way of living going forward.

Becoming more accepting of and in tune with who you are will benefit your overall confidence and self-esteem. It was through self-awareness that I was able to identify my destructive relationship patterns and make changes that set me up for healthier relationships.

Here's an exercise you can do to help with self-reflection. In order for it to be effective, you have to be honest with your responses. Free yourself from judgment and criticism, and answer from the heart.

Answer the following questions:

- What are some things that make you happy and sad, and why?
- How do you handle conflict?
- What are some of your achievements in life, and what did you learn about yourself from them? What about your disappointments?
- What are some things that motivate you, and why?
- Are you an introvert, an extrovert, or ambivert? Write down instances when you've exhibited behaviors that demonstrate your personality type.

✳ Download the Self-Awareness worksheet at www.youwereborntoheal.com/resources. ✳

Own Your Part

Does one person shoulder all the blame for a divorce? Maybe in some cases, depending on who you ask, but I believe the majority of divorces are the result of two people whose shortcomings and imperfections got the best of the marriage in some way. Not necessarily equally, but in a way that contributed to its ending.

Whether you initiated the divorce or not, there were certain things that did or didn't happen, things that were said or not said, on both sides during the marriage to keep it together. Maybe you were too controlling, not supportive enough, or unwilling to compromise on issues that were important to your partner, failing to meet their needs. You may not have spent enough quality time with your partner, or communicated effectively, or maybe you went into the marriage with trust issues that became insurmountable.

Depending on how and when your marriage ended, identifying the role you may have played in the marriage's demise might not be easy. Even still, you have to try to find where you contributed and take responsibility for it. I don't suggest you do this to chastise, shame, or point fingers at yourself, but rather to bring awareness of characteristics within yourself that may lead to similar situations in future relationships. Remember, this is about your transformation and preparing you for the future.

Awareness is key. With it comes a choice in how you want to approach life situations going forward. Do you want to make certain changes in an effort to get different results? Is that just who you are, and people will have to accept you for it? The decision is yours.

To help you see whatever part you may have played in the divorce, think about your marriage in its entirety and answer the following questions. The more honest you are with your answers, the more effective this exercise will be for you.

- Did you bring any unresolved issues from previous relationships into your marriage? If yes, what ways did they manifest themselves in your marriage?
- What were some of your ex's complaints about you? Think about what they might say to a marriage counselor about you. Have you heard similar complaints in past relationships, intimate or otherwise?
- How did those complaints impact your marriage? Think about how your ex said they felt afterwards or how their behavior changed as a result of this source of their complaints. What was the impact to them? (Note: If you

were the victim of gaslighting or other manipulation tactics, please keep that in mind as you answer these questions. This should not become an avenue for you to take on someone else's negative comments about you as your new beliefs. Use your judgment to distinguish between criticism based in fact and criticism used to control you.)

- Did you make any adjustments or changes as a result of those complaints? If yes, how did they help, if at all?
- What can you do better next time? Now that you've identified whatever part you played and how that impacted your marriage, decide what, if anything, you're willing to do to prevent this from happening again.

Shortly after my divorce was final, while I was still healing but in a much better place, mentally and emotionally, I became curious about other people's divorce experiences. Did we all go through some of the same things? Were our lives impacted in similar ways? How long did it take them to heal, and how did they go about doing so? Answers to these questions would help me to gauge where I was along my journey and give me different perspectives on how to move forward in a transformative way.

To find answers, I conducted a survey of forty men and women who'd been married anywhere from 8 months to 31 years before their divorce. One of the questions I asked them was: "If you got married again, what would you do differently to make the marriage work?"

Here's some of what they said.

"Being honest about how things make me feel in our relationship, no matter how upsetting it may be for either of us." – Mike M.

"Make sure there is a viable, passionate connection and that we have similar interests." – Ryan A.

"Make sure we can communicate properly, even if that means premarital counseling. Be friends. Listen to my gut. Don't marry expecting the other person to change." – Dayna L.

"Address issues head-on and be more vocal with my feelings." – Tiffani W.

"If I were to marry again, I would want to maintain open communication with my partner and make an effort to sustain the intimacy/passion between us." – Allisa J.

"I wouldn't marry a man based on his potential. I'd only marry him if I knew that I could be happy with him just as he was."

– Althia M.

"More communication and togetherness. Make marriage a team effort. And the team should only be the two of you, not all family members." – Brandon B.

"I would communicate my feelings more. I was always so worried about rocking the boat with my ex that sometimes I wouldn't say anything" – Felicia B.

"I would communicate my feelings and concerns with my mate when an issue arises rather than bottling them up inside. I can't control another person's actions, but I can let them know how it affects me and our relationship." – Sharlene K.

"I would verbally communicate about all aspects of life, truly gain understanding of each other, and come to agreements/compromises and stand by them." – Sam W.

"Put God first. Minimize routine in my relationship, and look for fun ways to keep things fresh and different." – Shamecka I.

"Number one, be happy with who I am and what I am about, and don't expect that validation from my spouse. Learn to be a better and more attentive listener and be patient in love as much as I am passionate in love." – Ish B.

"Identify my past faults and try to improve them. Also try to be more understanding." – Shatire P.

Can you relate to any of these responses? What would you add to this list of doing things differently if I asked you the same question? Notice how most of the responses center around some form of communication.

One of the things I would encourage you to do early on in the divorce process is spend time alone. Avoid jumping into another serious relationship until you've had time to reflect back on your relationship journey. Use that alone time to become more aware of the decisions you make and why when it comes to intimate relationships.

After my last relationship ended, I felt like I had just gone through another divorce. After the time we'd spent together, the friendships we'd established, and the bonding of our kids all ended, I needed some quality time alone to focus on myself. This was something I hadn't done enough of since my divorce. When it came to intimate relationships, I didn't want to create any more pain for myself or the people who were impacted by the break-ups.

During this time, I created my own version of a spiritual cleansing. I avoided some of the physical pleasures I had grown accustomed to, including sex and any form of intimacy that might lead to an emotional connection. That wasn't easy. I also didn't date anyone seriously. I wanted to minimize as many distractions as possible, and I didn't need anything or anyone clouding my judgment. As a result, I gained mental clarity and was able to unwind residual soul ties that I had created over the years.

That clarity was what I needed to do an effective self-assessment.

I reviewed this last serious relationship, my marriage with my ex-wife, as well as associations with former girlfriends. Why had none of these relationships lasted? Did I not try hard enough to keep us together? I was the common denominator, so was there something within me that needed to change? Until that time, I had been too busy playing the victim role to focus on my own transgressions. One of the things I uncovered about myself was that I had never learned how to prepare for a successful, healthy relationship, which I will show you how to do later in this book.

In addition to the trust issues that stemmed from my relationship with my father, there were two "egotistical" characteristics within me that impacted my ability to maintain a healthy relationship. They are common traits among other divorcees I've talked to and coached, and might be familiar to you.

One is placing more emphasis on the physical than the mental and emotional. I based some of my early choices of partners on

> " What are some things going on within that may be causing you to go without? "

what I saw on the outside, which heavily influenced my actions and behaviors. This stemmed partly from my environment growing up and what I was exposed to by the media and my social circles.

Looks were the initial attraction, which is not uncommon for a lot of people, especially men who tend to be more physically driven. Most people are physically attracted to the person they date in some way, at least in the beginning. Nobody wants a "mudduck," I often say jokingly, if you can imagine what a duck in the mud looks like.

However, when what you see trumps what you feel, when the physical outweighs the mental and emotional in such a way that it blinds you to warning signs and other compatibility issues, you run a high risk of the relationship not working out down the road. Ignoring those issues, thinking they'll eventually go away or the person will change, carries with it the same, if not a slightly higher, risk of failure.

It clouded my judgment in certain cases, and led me to make decisions based on superficial things instead of matters of substance. My focus on looks often made it difficult to establish an organic connection in the beginning.

I shared this story with one of my clients, Lou, who was experiencing something similar. He'd been "blinded by beauty" in his past relationships, paying more attention to what he saw on the outside than what he felt on the inside. Being seen with a certain type of woman was a status symbol that he believed made him look good, despite the emotional disconnect he often felt inside. This led to constant arguments behind closed doors.

I had one of those "doing the same things over again and expecting different results" conversations with him, and I encouraged him to step outside his comfort zone by relaxing some of the physical requirements he had in place. In order to do this, I asked him to rank those physical must-haves in order of importance, and identify some adjustments he could make, especially for those characteristics that ranked lower on his list. Not only did his dating options increase, but he also found that a lot of the connection points with the women outside of his "perfect mold" were stronger.

My other harmful behavior was focusing more on what potential partners didn't have or weren't bringing to the relationship, instead of what they did bring to the relationship. The 80/20 rule. Their lack or faults overshadowed everything else, despite those being of lower value in comparison to what they did bring to the table. I was seeking perfection, despite my own imperfections, which was a selfish act on my part. Not only did these characteristics keep my relationships from thriving and lasting, but they also created self-esteem and trust issues in some of the women I dated. This was an unintentional but very real consequence.

Self-Reflection: Identify Relationship Patterns

Self-reflection is an important part of the healing process because it gives you an opportunity to make adjustments for future relationships by looking at the ones from your past. By identifying relationship patterns, you're making a connection between the dating choices you've made, and any commonalities that contributed to their success or failure.

The first part of this self-reflection exercise looks at life before marriage. The following questions will help you identify relationship patterns you've developed over time that may have contributed to your divorce in some way.

Be as descriptive as possible in your answers to these questions:

- What patterns do you notice when you think about your past relationships, including your marriage? Think about specific situations that took place and how you responded.
- Highlight or circle the patterns you feel are problematic.
- For each pattern you identified as problematic, describe why it's a problem.
- Did you bring any of those problematic patterns into your marriage? If so, what impact did they have on your marriage?
- Are there any other people within your family that have exhibited similar patterns?

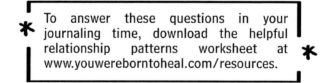

To answer these questions in your journaling time, download the helpful relationship patterns worksheet at www.youwereborntoheal.com/resources.

How It Ended

How did your initial vision of marriage differ from the reality of your marriage? To get a better understanding of why your marriage ended and what role you may have played, it often helps to start from the beginning. Think back to when you first said, "I do." What was the state of your relationship at that point?

Was your marriage happy and stable from the start? Why or why not? Did one of you come into the relationship with emotional baggage from a prior relationship? If it was you, in what ways did this baggage manifest itself in your marriage, and what was the result?

Did your dating relationship differ from your marriage relationship? If so, how? What triggered the change? Were your actions and behaviors consistent between the two phases? Consistency is important. What you did to win your spouse's hand in marriage should continue into the marriage. While change is a natural occurrence, there are certain behaviors that should continue. If they don't and are not discussed, this could lead to divorce.

Describe the turning point when things began to go downhill. What role did you play, if any? Some changes are gradual. They may have started out small and seemed insignificant, but over time became more impactful. How did you handle the change as it began to unfold? How did it make you feel? What were some of the challenges you faced and how did you handle them? What was the sequence of events that transpired? After all, a divorce can be traced back to a sequence of events that takes place during the marriage.

What was the straw that broke the camel's back? In other words, what was the particular challenge that happened that the two of you were unable to move past. Describe what led to the demise of the marriage. Do not complete this exercise with the attitude of blaming your ex for everything. There were two players in your game, and one of them was you, so take responsibility.

Visualize the Future

Depending on where you are on your emotional journey, visualizing what your next relationship or marriage might be like could be difficult. Another relationship, let alone marriage, might be the last thing on your mind. And that's fine for now. However, I want you to begin planting seeds of hope. Part of the healing process is to be able to see beyond your current situation and look towards a brighter future. This exercise will help you to do just that. It's not meant to keep you so focused on the future that you miss the journey, but rather to help you close the gap between where you are now and where you want to be, one day at a time.

Clear your mind. Imagine that you've healed from your divorce and you're thinking about marriage again, only this time with more insight and awareness. You've assessed your mental state and owned the part you played in the demise of your marriage. You've identified the characteristics you want in a spouse. You're more in tune with what brings you joy and happiness. What does marriage look like for you this time? How do you and your spouse start and end most days together, and what are you doing for leisure? What's your communication like and how do you resolve issues? What's your intimacy like, including sex? What challenges might you face? How will the two of you work through them? What are some of the quirky things about you that they'll have to put up with?

When the time is right, use these answers as a way to attract the relationship you want. Consider this your relationship vision board, designed to set the tone for your path forward. I'm a firm believer in the law of attraction, so use this vision in support of that. Allow God and the spiritual energy associated with focus to handle the rest.

Begin to live the life that you envision with your significant other as much as possible. If you see the two of you traveling together, then incorporate traveling into your current routine now. If you imagine the two of you talking honestly about conflicts or areas of disagreement, resolve conflicts in life now through proper communication the way you would in your intimate relationships. The more you begin to live this life the more real it will become for you.

Mistakes to Avoid

While it's important to look back at how things went wrong, don't make the mistake of dwelling on what happened in your marriage. This will only cause unnecessary pain and suffering, which we'll talk more about in the next chapter. It's normal, especially in the beginning, to spend time thinking about the divorce, but begin to limit your time there. And when you do think about the past, reflect on what happened as a way to prepare you for the future.

Avoid being overly critical or judgmental of yourself and your ex. Whether you initiated the divorce or not, whether you were the root cause or the victim, harsh criticism gives power to something you can't change. This will only add to your pain and suffering, taking up valuable space that could be used for growth. It's only natural for you to be emotional, but don't let that consume you.

Use the experience to bring more awareness of yourself as

a person. Allow the mistakes made and lessons learned to serve as a guide for who you want to become, not a sentencing or negative description of who you were. It's a more productive use of your time, especially since you can't change what happened. You now have a starting point for healing and growth.

Chapter 2.

The Wound:
Your Emotional Journey

Divorce is an emotionally taxing process that can impact multiple areas of your life. Much like the physical wound I suffered on my hand, the wounds you experience from a divorce can come with various forms of emotional pain—anger, resentment, fear, guilt, shame, embarrassment, bitterness, confusion, and the list goes on. I didn't realize how much so until I went through my own divorce. Outside of my mom's death, no other experience in my years of living can compare. And I'm prayerful it stays that way.

That pain often comes in waves, depending on the day, and hits its peak in the early stages of a divorce, which are often the most challenging. This is when you are most vulnerable and subject to high levels of sensitivity. It doesn't take much to send you into a tizzy or invoke mood swings, as you wrestle with the realities of your situation and try to find some sense of normalcy in a world that suddenly seems upside-down.

Going through a divorce can have you acting out of character or saying or doing things you ordinarily wouldn't, and may later regret. It's not just the marriage that's impacted, but all areas of life, including your job, family, social circles, and spiritual life.

It can take some people years to heal and move on with their lives, while others never do. Some think they are healed only to find out that they're not, which can make things worse. If this is what you are experiencing, realize that it's a natural part of the healing process; an unwanted necessity that divorcees often go through in order to heal.

Some people have equated the emotional experience of divorce with that of the death of a loved one. The journey of processing a divorce follows a similar pattern as Elisabeth Kübler-Ross's "five stages of grief" model, which identifies denial, anger, bargaining, depression, and acceptance as the stages that people go through when a loved one is dying or has already passed on.

Below is an adaptation of that model[3] as it relates to divorce. Knowing where you are on your divorce journey can help you identify what needs to be done to get to a place of healing.

Denial: People in this stage tend to downplay what's really happening. They may try to paint a picture to the world that everything is okay, or they continue to operate as if they are still happily married. A bit of disbelief comes into play, with statements like, "This can't be happening, not to me."

Anger: People in this stage come to the realization that they can no longer deny what's happening. Anger and other emotions

---

3   Elisabeth Krübler-Ross, *On Death and Dying* (New York: The Macmillan Company, 1969).

are heightened, which may lead to mood swings and irrational behavior. They may say things like, "Why me?" or "It's not fair," or "How could this be happening to me?"

Bargaining: Despite knowing the marriage's ultimate fate, people in this stage hope they can delay the divorce for as long as possible, sometimes to the dismay of their estranged spouse. They may pray to whatever higher power they worship for more time in exchange for a change in behavior. They may say or do things to stay in the separation phase as long as possible.

Grief: Reality has set in that divorce is inevitable, resulting in deep sadness and sorrow. A person in this stage may want to be left alone to process those feelings and mourn the loss of their marriage. They may begin to lose hope for a brighter future. An extended grief period can lead to depression.

Acceptance: People in this stage have accepted that the marriage is over. They are ready to put the divorce behind them and move on with their life. There is a level of peace and understanding with their new reality, which opens the door for healing and transformation.

A lot of divorcees I talk to follow this pattern of behavior, including one of my clients, Sheila, who went through a divorce after more than twenty years of marriage. She had operated in a state of comfort in her dysfunctional marriage for years, and she was finally ready to get out. However, she and her husband had been married for so long that they both found it hard to accept that the divorce was even happening.

For several months after she said she wanted out, they continued taking care of each other, making sure needs were met as if the conversation had never taken place. They continued to attend family events together, and she'd even check in with him at times when she was on vacation. A part of her considered it just a rough patch in their marriage, one that they'd eventually get through. The big "D" word had been hinted at before, but nothing had ever happened.

It wasn't until she decided to move out that reality began to set in, which was hard for her to accept at times. What she once envisioned for her life, her marriage, was fading away, which led to various forms of pain, including anger, bitterness, regret, sadness, fear, and confusion. That pain and how she experienced it varied from day to day. There were times when she felt right about the move she was making to leave and other times when she didn't.

She even considered going back a time or two after conversations with her estranged husband about a change in behavior on his part. His actions continued to say something different, however, so she didn't. As they spent more time apart and she began to live the life she wanted, she came to accept the fact that the marriage was over. She began to realize that she was happier and more fulfilled without him, and that they could both operate as a healthy unit when it came to raising their kids. Her acceptance of the divorce was when she began to grow and transform into a new person who continues to evolve with time.

Your emotional journey may be different from the one described above, but the impact tends to be the same. What you say and do, how you think and feel, who you associate with—all these things are impacted by a divorce. The more invested you were in the marriage, the stronger the bond you had with your spouse, the more intensely you'll feel your emotional wounds.

Wounds hurt the most when they first happen, which is why the early stages of a divorce are the most difficult to endure mentally and emotionally. At times, you'll feel like you're on an emotional roller coaster. One day, you may be fueled with anger and just want to be alone, and the next day, you may feel sad and need someone to talk to about what you're experiencing.

The emotions you experience and to what extent you experience them largely depend on you as a person and the circumstances behind your divorce. If you initiated the divorce, for example, you may feel a sense of relief as well as sadness. You may be relieved that you are no longer in a marriage that was toxic but sad that your family structure is broken. If you didn't, you may experience anger or resentment. Depending on the day, you may feel some of these emotions more than others. You may even go back and forth between different emotions throughout the day.

These wounds can run deep and wide, impacting other areas of your personal and professional life as well. My work performance suffered during my divorce, and I ended up unemployed for a couple of months. How long that journey lasts, how long you continue to experience these emotions, depends a lot on you and the steps you take to heal.

With divorce can come a loss of self. Not necessarily a complete loss, but one that requires you to explore within and identify who you are as an individual outside of your marriage. You may have spent so much of your time and energy trying to keep the marriage alive and healthy that you forgot about the things that truly made you happy and fulfilled.

The longer you were married, the more your identity may have been tied to the marriage. You may have lived a life that your spouse wanted you to, or you may have gone along with certain decisions for the sake of the relationship, not because you wanted to. Maybe you didn't have much of a social life outside of your partner. Their friends became your friends. Now that you're no longer married, you're confused, lonely, and at a loss for how to move forward.

The most enlightening part of my emotional journey was learning about the mental-emotional connection. Not only did it help me to manage the emotions I experienced from my divorce, but it also laid the foundation for my overall growth and transformation.

Understanding how your emotions work and learning how to manage them is an essential part of the healing process. Managing emotions is challenging for a lot of people, especially in the early stages of their divorce. If you naturally struggle with controlling your emotions in everyday situations, divorce brings an additional layer of complexity. I recommend my clients incorporate learning to manage their emotions in their self-care routine throughout their emotional journey.

Here are six of the most common emotions experienced while going through a divorce, according to the divorcees I surveyed:

Anger. Some were angry at their spouse for what they did or failed to do. Others were angry at themselves for staying in the marriage too long or for getting married in the first place despite the warning signs. One woman said she was angry with God, despite her strong spiritual background and beliefs.

Loneliness. Everything from being in a house that was suddenly minus one, to participating in activities or going to functions alone, and no longer having the same level of intimacy readily available caused loneliness. This was often the case even for people who had been unhappy in their marriage. Those who no longer came home to their kids on a regular basis felt an emptiness inside, a longing for the hugs and unconditional love their children showed them.

Embarrassment. Some of the respondents had gotten married despite pleas from family or friends not to, and now they had to "eat crow." One man, whose marriage looked perfect on the outside, felt embarrassed when people found out he and his wife were getting a divorce. He'd given off the impression that all was well in the relationship, but now people could see it was struggling and had failed. For some, this was their second failed marriage, which made them feel even more embarrassed. All sorts of societal taboos about divorce can contribute to this embarrassment.

Fear. Not knowing what to expect after divorce was scary for some people. Financially and romantically, they weren't sure which direction their life was headed in, which led to fear. One woman, who'd been married twenty-five years, wasn't sure how to operate independent of her marriage, which contributed to her fear.

Resentment. Many respondents resented what felt like time wasted and broken promises. Some felt like they'd given the marriage their all, but their ex hadn't put forth the same amount of effort in return. Both a woman and a man resented their ex-spouse for misleading them about who they were prior to the marriage.

Sadness. Many respondents felt deep sadness over the love lost or the promise of a lifetime together that failed to come to fruition. It's not unusual to feel sad about a divorce even when you're the one who initiated it.

Although these emotions and others are natural for a lot of divorcees, dwelling in these negative emotional states is not healthy. It causes unnecessary pain and suffering.

If you're struggling to move past certain emotions, here are some questions you can answer to understand the source of those emotions and how to overcome them:

- What emotion(s) are you wrestling with as a result of your divorce?
- What thought(s) are you having that are fueling those emotions, keeping them alive?
- Besides keeping the emotional experience alive, what

purpose do those thoughts serve?

- Are these thoughts beneficial to you in any way?
- Knowing you can't change what's already happened, what's the silver lining in your divorce situation, and how can that help you move forward?

Understand Your Emotions

Stacey was fresh out of her marriage and an emotional wreck when she came to me for help. Her soon-to-be ex-husband was about to get half the equity from the sale of their house, despite not contributing anything financially to its purchase. She'd paid the mortgage, so she didn't think it was fair that he was about to get so much. Legally, there was nothing she could do about it, however, since his name was on the deed.

She thought he was about to get an unjustified "come up," which made her feel used and foolish. Constant thoughts of him "stealing" her money and showing off her hard work to others with a new car, another house, and other fancy purchases played out in her head, which only made her more upset. Those thoughts added to the pain and frustration she was dealing with from other issues related to the divorce, and they drained her energy and motivation.

I helped Stacey understand what she was experiencing emotionally had less to do with the money and more to do with the narrative she was creating in her mind. The fact that he was getting half the money had already been decided and agreed upon. Her mental expectations of what he should get conflicted with what he was actually getting, and she was refusing to accept that reality. She was creating her own anger and bitterness by not accepting what she couldn't change and continuing to dwell on it. She was choosing not to let it go mentally, thus keeping the pain alive emotionally. I wasn't discounting what Stacey was feeling, but rather bringing awareness into the why.

In his book *The Power of Now*, Eckhart Tolle discusses how an "emotion arises at the place where mind and body meet. It's the body's reaction to the mind."[4] We generate emotions based on our thought processes, both conscious and unconscious, at the time. He goes on to say the more identified we are with our thinking—our likes, dislikes, judgments, interpretations—the stronger our emotional reaction will be. In other words, if someone does or says something that goes against what you expect or firmly believe, the intensity level of what you feel within will be magnified. In Stacey's case, she was adding to her existing pain and suffering from the divorce by adding the financial situation to the mix, creating a snowball effect.

This link between mind and body, your thoughts and emotions, is an important concept to understand. It's a pivotal part of the healing process and your emotional wellness, and one of the most powerful transformation tools you have available. It will serve as the foundation for learning how to manage your emotions on this emotional journey.

To illustrate this link further, I want you to do an exercise with me. Close your eyes and think about a recent experience you had with someone or something, whether positive or negative. Stay there for sixty seconds and really home in on that experience as if it were happening again, right now. Watch it unfold as if it were playing out on your mental movie screen. Do those thoughts evoke any emotions? If so, what are they?

If you chose to think about an experience your mind deemed positive, you probably felt positive emotions like happiness or joy. You may have even found yourself smiling as a result of those thoughts. The opposite holds true if you thought about

---

4   Eckhart Tolle, *Practicing The Power of Now: Essential Teachings, Meditations, and Exercises From The Power of Now*, (Novato, California: New World Library, 1997) p. 24.

something negative that happened. Your body may have tensed up as a result. Even though the situation wasn't actually happening, your mind made it real and your emotions followed. There is no difference between the real and the remembered. The body reacts based on what the mind creates.

You can practice connecting your thoughts and emotions by bringing awareness into what you feel in your body and asking, "What am I thinking about?" You can also bring awareness into your subconscious thoughts by identifying your current mood or how you feel right now. You may not always realize what you're thinking about, but you will always feel it. Doing this will help you identify the source of what's causing you to feel a certain way.

When I talk to divorcees about the source of their pain and emotional turmoil, they often point back to specific situations. I hear comments like: "My ex did or didn't do this." "My finances are ruined." "I won't be able to see my kids every day." They attribute their feelings to something that happened to them, and to a certain extent, they are right. Had these things not happened, there's a good chance they wouldn't be riding this current emotional roller coaster. However, once events happen, they no longer serve as the emotional source. Compulsive thinking about them does. Reliving the past keeps you there, not only in thought but in actions as well. This can hinder your healing.

Through a series of questions, Stacey came to the conclusion that her emotional wounds were primarily driven by two things in particular at the time. One was no longer having a family structure. Thoughts of being a wife and serving as a mother to her stepchildren, to whom she'd become very attached, were causing her to feel sad and lonely. When she couldn't talk to the children, she would often get upset, and when she could, her spirits were uplifted.

The other driver was feeling like she'd been used and manipulated by her husband, thoughts that made her angry and bitter. She was upset not just about the money situation, but also about the way he made her look like the bad and crazy person in front of other people. Thoughts about the two issues drained her mentally and physically. She stopped working out and stayed in the house more than usual.

The story you create in your mind about your situation is the primary source of your emotions. It's what causes you to feel the way you do. What your ex did or didn't do, said or failed to say, none of that truly matters anymore because it already happened. You can't change it. Yet, you continue to energize it and give it life by giving it psychological time, or time spent dwelling on past and future. Maybe the situation bruised your ego, or maybe your self-image was threatened. Either way, your mind won't let it go, so you continue to experience the emotions associated with the thoughts. The same holds true with any thoughts you have about what could've been had the two of you been able to work things out and keep the marriage together.

Let's do an exercise similar to the one we did before, only this time I don't want you to think about anything at all. Instead, find a comfortable position to sit in. Close your eyes and take a few deep breaths. Clear your mind of any thoughts and just listen to what's going on around you. Don't try to interpret, judge, or analyze what you hear, as that will create mind activity. Just focus on the sounds and allow them to come and go naturally. If any thoughts creep in, take notice of them, then bring your attention back to what you hear.

You can also do this exercise by bringing attention to what you feel—your butt in the seat, your feet on the floor, the life energy flowing through your body. As with the sounds, if any thoughts creep in, bring your attention back to what you're feeling. Do this for sixty seconds.

✳ BE PRESENT

You can practice mindlessness in multiple ways and places. Take brushing your teeth, for example. Instead of thinking about what happened yesterday or what needs to be done later, feel the bristles moving against your teeth, your gums, your tongue. Feel the sensation in your hand and arm as you guide the toothbrush around in your mouth. Taste the toothpaste. Feel the water swishing around when you rinse.

When driving, turn the radio off for a few minutes and listen to what's going on around you—the tires against the road, the engine, other cars and trucks passing by. Feel your hands on the steering wheel, your back and butt against the seat, the vibration of the car as you drive down the road. Let the windows down and hear and feel the wind blowing. What other sounds can you hear inside or outside of your car?

As you walk outside, what do you hear? Birds chirping? Dogs barking? Airplanes flying overhead or music from cars in the distance? Notice the smells and the trees and the buildings you pass by as you continue walking.

Remember, as you're doing these activities, don't try to interpret, question, guess, analyze, or judge what's going on, as those actions involve your mind. Instead, bring awareness into what's happening around you by using your senses. Focus all your attention on the activity itself as if you were hearing, seeing, feeling, tasting, and smelling for the first time. In other words, be present.

Did you experience any emotions when you were focused on sounds or sensations? If so, what were they? If you didn't feel anything, or you felt a sense of peace and calm, and you were free of worry and stress, then you were able to access the power of being present without creating any negative emotions from past or future by thinking.

I encourage you to practice this mindlessness exercise multiple times per day, throughout your day, as part of your self-care routine. Start with a short time, like sixty seconds, and increase the length of time from there. Two minutes, five minutes, ten minutes. Every time you find your mind wandering, center yourself by refocusing on your senses. The more you practice this, the wider the mental gap between thinking and non-thinking will become.

For many people, being present for extended periods of time isn't an easy thing to do. If that's you, maybe you've been taught since childhood to constantly think, so your thoughts and mind activity have tremendous momentum. Making exercises like these a habit will give you a break from the incessant mental noise that dictates so much of your emotions. It will strengthen your ability to stay present, to stop dwelling on what you can't control (past and future), and to focus on what you can control (present). It will help the cycle of pain you may be experiencing from your divorce. Consciously or unconsciously, influential people in our lives convinced us to think a certain way, and that helps shape the narrative we form to respond in certain situations. A mindlessness practice allows you to disengage from that narrative.

Mental resistance to "what is" or "what was" is a major source of emotional pain and suffering. This happens when your expectations about what should or shouldn't have happened or what someone did or didn't do are not aligned with reality.

Said a different way, something didn't go according to plan or how you thought it would and you've yet to accept or let go of that mentally. In your mind, you still believe there's an action you can take to alter or influence something that has already happened, and that's not possible.

If you find yourself in a situation that you are unable to change or remove yourself from, accept it as if you had chosen it. Then take whatever action is necessary from there to move forward. Any mental resistance to what happened at this point will only create unnecessary pain and suffering that's also counterproductive to forward progress.

Let's say you're driving down the road and get a flat tire. If you refuse to accept the fact that you have a flat tire, then you are creating unnecessary pain and suffering. Why? Because you can't change the fact that you have a flat tire. You may naturally get upset, curse, yell, kick the tire, or otherwise express anger or frustration as your initial emotional reaction, but to dwell in that emotional state and not accept the reality of the situation is pointless. It's keeping you stuck. Instead, respond to the situation from there. Change the tire or call a tow truck. Take some sort of productive action instead of creating further emotional turmoil.

As you become more aware of your emotions, you will most likely find you have an active thought process going on about something that happened in the past or might happen in the future. A mindlessness practice can keep the pain and suffering at bay by taking your mind off the past, what happened to your marriage and what may happen to you going forward. Be alert to the rising of your emotions in everyday situations. If someone cuts you off on the highway, insults you on social media, or interrupts you at work, recognize your feelings the moment they begin to happen. Feel them bubbling up inside and tie your thoughts back to them. With awareness comes a choice of how you respond, as opposed to being unaware and falling back into the same emotional reactive patterns.

Remember your emotions and thoughts energize each other. The thought enjoys the energy it receives from the emotion, which creates similar thoughts to keep you in that emotional state. Once it starts, this back-and-forth cycle can continue for minutes, hours, or days. It has tremendous momentum. Positive thoughts generate positive emotions, and negative thoughts generate more of the same, as illustrated in the exercise you did earlier.

In our early times together, Stacey would often talk about how hurt and sad she felt because she missed her stepchildren. The thought of them no longer being in her life led to feelings of anger, as she focused on her husband's failure to contribute financially to the purchase of the house and the fact that he would still reap a substantial financial reward from its sale. That conversation begot one about how he'd acted as if their marriage was perfect in public, giving people advice on how to make their relationships better, but didn't practice what he preached in their marriage, which made her more upset. The children were the initial spark. Everything she felt from there spiraled towards the negative as a result of her thoughts.

The feeling you get from a thought can be unconsciously addictive. This keeps the mental-emotional cycle going even though you're unaware of it. That's one of the reasons why it's easy to get caught up in an argument. This also holds true for the positive or negative energy you receive from other people. Think about your interactions with people and how they make you feel. Some people bring positive energy, which rubs off of you. The same holds true for people with negative energy. This is why you have to be careful of the people you surround yourself with, especially during a divorce when you're already more emotional.

Triggers

Emotional triggers are those situations that cause an intense emotional reaction, regardless of your current mood. This can include memories, certain topics, another person's words or actions, and even your own behavior. Knowing your triggers and how to deal with them is a key component of your emotional health.

We all have certain emotional triggers. Some common ones include:

- rejection
- betrayal
- challenged beliefs
- disapproval or criticism
- being excluded or ignored
- unjust treatment

Learning how to recognize your triggers requires listening to your mind and body. What are you telling yourself, and how are you reacting? You may experience a variety of physical symptoms like a racing heart, sweaty palms, or shakiness.

Your triggers are often the result of events from your childhood, how you were raised, something traumatic that happened in your life, or your self-image being challenged or threatened in some way. A great example of the latter is Marty McFly in the movie *Back to the Future*. Anytime someone called him "chicken," a switch would flip inside. He'd go from a mild-mannered, nonconfrontational guy, to someone ready to fight.

Approach your triggers with curiosity to get more insight on their root cause. Do any patterns stand out? Are there other situations that make you feel the same way? Feeling the energy behind the emotions as they bubble up inside gives you a choice on how to respond. There's a window of time, albeit small in most cases, during which you're conscious enough to determine your next move. This can lead to a more favorable response, or at least one you intend, as opposed to being unconscious and reacting in a way you may later regret. As you become more aware of your triggers and your mind activity surrounding your divorce, you gain better control of your emotions.

Methods to Manage Your Emotions

Now that I've given you some insight into how emotions work, let's look at some ways to help you manage them. For a lot of people, it's much easier to understand the source of emotions than it is to manage them. This is where most of my clients struggle, just as I did, especially early on in the divorce.

Managing your emotions is all about self-regulation or your ability to experience thoughts and emotions and choose a response from there. It's a learned skill that requires practice, time, patience, and more practice. Awareness is also a foundational component.

The way you handle your emotions has a lot to do with your upbringing. According to licensed psychologist Pauline Peck, PhD, the way our parents and caregivers model emotional management, as well as the messages they give us about our emotions, can have a tremendous impact on how we understand our emotions and whether we believe we can handle them.[5] People who didn't experience a supportive environment in early childhood, for example, may have a more difficult time with emotional regulation than those who did. Emotions are a normal and natural part of how you respond to situations.

---

5   Hilary I. Lebow, "6 Ways to Manage Your Emotions and Improve Your Mood," PsychCentral. com, April 12, 2022, https://psychcentral.com/health/ways-to-manage-your-emotions

They can provide you with valuable information about yourself and what's going on in your life, so they shouldn't be denied or suppressed. Doing so will only create further pain and suffering that will manifest itself in some way later down the line. Accept what you feel without judging or criticizing yourself for it. Use therapist-backed strategies, like the ones that follow, to help you effectively manage your emotions.

Sensory grounding is a practice of focusing on your senses, similar to my earlier example. This is an effective way to break the cycle of negative thinking and stay present. In addition to the mindlessness exercise, I encourage my clients to practice a popular grounding exercise called the 5-4-3-2-1 technique. Focus on: five things you see, four things you feel, three things you hear, two things you smell, and one thing you taste. Do your best to stay present while engaging in these grounding exercises. If it helps, experience everything as if it's the first time. Try not to label, judge, analyze, question, or interpret. When thoughts creep in, refocus by coming back to your senses.

Research suggests that **deep breathing** activates the parasympathetic nervous system, which allows your body to unwind and restore balance. Box breathing is a popular exercise you can do to help with this. Try this several times until you feel a sense of calmness. Inhale while counting to four. Hold for four counts. Exhale for four counts. Hold for four counts. Repeat. While the emotion may not go away completely, deep breathing exercises can help prevent extreme emotional reactions you want to avoid.

Meditation. According to an article in *Behavior Brain Research*, a daily meditation practice of thirteen minutes over the course of eight weeks helped improve people's mood and emotional regulation. It also provided additional benefits such as enhanced attention and memory.

Seek professional help. If you are unable to manage your emotions on your own, it may be beneficial to seek the services of a therapist or coach. Find a professional who can help you process your emotions in a healthy way.

To recap, there are several key points to remember when it comes to understanding and managing emotions that stem from your divorce. First, be aware of your emotional triggers. Feel the emotion bubbling up inside when you find yourself in a situation that invokes emotion. Awareness gives you a choice in how you respond, so you can choose to react rationally. Be alert to situations that might provoke a reaction of some sort.

Second, check your narrative. It's not the situation, but rather the mental commentary you're creating about it, that generates the emotion. The situation is what it is, so be mindful of the narrative you're creating. Is this an ego thing?

Third, practice acceptance. Mental resistance to what's already happened creates unnecessary pain and suffering. If there's nothing you can do to change the situation, then manage your emotions by accepting it. Surrender to what is, then shift your focus to how you're going to move forward from it.

Fourth, control time. Manage your emotions by controlling the amount of time you spend thinking about past and future. If you're dwelling on your divorce, you're taking time away from the present moment and how that can be used to move you forward. Remember this: The future is only a thought in your mind. You create it daily through present moment activities.

Mistakes to Avoid

Learning how to manage your emotions after divorce takes more time for some people than others. It can be especially challenging for those who've struggled with emotional regulation in the past, but with effort, we can all improve in this area. As you develop this skill, avoid the following obstacles.

Addictive pleasures. Avoid relying on addictive pleasures like drugs or alcohol to cope with your emotions. They will only mask the pain, providing a temporary sense of relief. Their numbing effects will eventually wear off, leaving you feeling the same way as before, if not worse. On top of that they are unhealthy, and their long-term effects can do more harm than good. If you are struggling in this area, please seek professional help as soon as possible.

Negative environment. Be mindful of the places you go, the people you associate with, and the things you listen to. You're already dealing with negativity from the divorce itself, so the last thing you want to do is add more negativity into the mix. Instead, surround yourself with people who will support and uplift you, and listen to and read things that inspire you in a positive, mentally healthy way.

Suppressing the pain. Emotions are a natural part of the human experience, so avoid trying to suppress or deny what you are feeling. Doing so can delay or prevent true healing and lead to unhealthy consequences both mentally and physically. Process your emotions instead, using the strategies outlined in this book. Talk to people you trust, join a divorce support group, journal, or seek professional help. It's important that you focus on your mental health on this journey.

Judging or being overly critical of yourself. Avoid judging yourself for how you feel. What you experience emotionally is unique to you, so don't get upset with yourself if you react irrationally to some trigger. Give yourself some grace instead. You've become conditioned to being who you are over the course of decades, so don't expect change to happen overnight. Take baby steps. You're still healing and this is part of the transformational process.

The strategies for managing your emotions take practice, consistency, and patience. With life-changing events like a divorce, we often spend a good portion of our time thinking about the past and future. Don't allow psychological time to consume you. Your instinct may be to react in a certain way to a situation without thought, only to realize how emotional you got some time after the fact. This is natural, so don't beat yourself up about it afterwards. That will only lead to more negativity.

The key for you will be to recognize when this happens and make note of what caused it. Go back and reread what I said earlier about the mental-emotional connection, and continue to practice managing your emotions. As you do, the time between when you react unconsciously again and when you realize it will become smaller. At some point, you will be able to feel yourself about to get emotional and be conscious of it before you fly off the deep end again. You'll respond without being drawn into whatever negative energy your mind is trying to feed on or create. This is a process. Although I'm much more aware of and in control of my emotions through several years of practice, I still find myself falling back into old reactive patterns from time to time.

Continue to practice the mindlessness activities shared here every day. Think about other routine activities you do, and incorporate these new exercises into your routine. When you listen to someone talk, or engage in an activity, be fully engaged. Use your senses to quiet your mind. Find and read books that focus on being present, such as *The Power of Now*.

Co-Parenting

As you go through a divorce, you have to adjust to new routines, like being single and dating again. You may have to take on additional household or financial responsibilities. If you and your ex have kids together, however, you also have to deal with co-parenting. This can be a challenge, especially if the relationship with your ex-spouse is contentious.

My ex-wife and I never had any major issues when it came to raising our son in separate households. Despite the fact that we didn't see eye to eye on certain things, our communication was broken, and we'd decided to go our separate ways, we agreed that we would never bad-mouth each other to our son. When we were all together, we were mindful of how we interacted with each other, despite how we may have felt about each other at the time. We wanted to be a unified front for the mental and emotional benefit of our child.

The success of this effort was made clear one day at a church event our son was participating in. He was young at the time, maybe four or five, and my ex and I both showed up for the event. We'd attended that church as a family for a while, but after the separation, my ex- wife decided to find another church to call home.

When the event was over, we walked out of the sanctuary together with our son walking in between us. All of a sudden, he grabbed one of her hands and one of mine. His face shone with joy, more than it had when he received an award just minutes earlier. Despite how uncomfortable I felt walking down the hall like that, I took *me* out of the equation as I watched him smile and skip along. I imagine my ex felt the same way I did because she didn't let go either.

How did we get to a point where we could put our son first? We focused on what was best for him. Before we decided to separate, when he was barely twenty-four months old, we agreed we didn't want to influence him in any way that might cause unfair resentment towards the other parent or ever force him to choose sides. We didn't want him to think that he was the cause of us going our separate ways. He was already going to grow up in two separate households, and only God knew what challenges our son might encounter in school and in life because his parents had divorced. We wanted to normalize as much as we could for him. This wasn't about money or our personal beliefs about each other and the divorce. It was about being united in the interest of our common denominator.

That same agreement continued throughout his childhood and adolescence. If his mother had an issue with him, she'd often call me first to see if she might be overreacting or to get my viewpoint as a man. I'd do the same when the situation was reversed and I wanted her thoughts as a woman and mother. We'd then have face-to-face discussions with him together. This worked for us because it's what we agreed on. Some divorcees with children aren't so fortunate.

Here are some tips to consider if you're dealing with a co-parenting situation:

1. Take you out of it. This is not about you or your ex, it's about your child and their overall well-being. Regardless of how you feel about your ex, the two of you have a child together who needs love and quality time from both parents. Don't influence your child in a negative way based on your own opinions and judgments about your ex.

2. Make co-parenting a team effort. While you and your ex may have different perspectives about life and how to live it, aim for consistency when it comes to certain rules and disciplinary actions. When my son lost TV or phone privileges at his mom's house, for example, I followed through with that punishment at my house. The same held true with certain rules like getting homework and household chores done, and going to bed at a certain time.

3. Communicate, communicate, communicate. I can't emphasize this enough. As tough as this may be, put your pride and ego to the side and make your child the focal point of conservations with your ex. Listen to your ex's viewpoints to gain understanding and respond from there. Come to an agreement based on what's in the best interest of your child.

According to the article, "Co-Parenting and Joint Custody Tips for Divorced Parents," kids whose divorced parents have a cooperative relationship:

- Feel more secure, adapt better to divorce and new living situations, and have better self-esteem.
- Benefit from consistency and knowing what to expect regardless of which parent they are with.
- Have a better understanding of how to solve problems effectively by watching the parents work together.
- Are mentally and emotionally healthier. [6]

While you can do your best to co-parent effectively, don't expect the process to be without difficulties. Despite our co-parenting agreement, I still faced some challenges as a divorced parent. I missed seeing my son every day, and holidays like Thanksgiving and Christmas are still tough when he's not with me. In the best circumstances, you and your ex will be similarly invested in parenting. However, if you feel your ex is not a good parent, let your child come to that conclusion on their own, without any negative influence from you. Don't muddy the water with your own personal beliefs, judgments, ill-feelings, or other negativity.

---

[6] Jocelyn Block, M.A. and Melinda Smith, M.A., "Co-Parenting and Joint Custody Tips for Divorced Parents," HelpGuide.org, accessed June 24, 2023, www. helpguide.org/articles/parenting-family/co- parenting-tips-for-divorced-parents.htm

Chapter 3.

The Scab:
Partner with Time to Heal

Scabs are not pretty. They have an amorphous appearance, are hard and rough around the edges, and have a distinct color that makes them stick out like a sore thumb. Despite their looks, however, we cannot heal properly without them. They serve as a natural barrier to external factors, such as germs and bacteria, that could otherwise infect the wound.

Underneath that protective layer is where the healing takes place. It's an inside-out process that happens over time, similar to the one divorcees need to adopt in order to heal their emotional wounds. These "emotional scabs" serve the same vital purpose as your physical ones. They create a safe environment that allows you to make changes from within yourself and grow at the same time, which is why they are such an essential part of your self-care routine.

A couple of questions I ask people who are having trouble healing and moving forward from their divorce are: "What are you doing to aid time in that process? How are you protecting your emotions and deepening your awareness of self along the way?"

Much like your physical wounds, the early stages of a divorce are when you are most vulnerable. Mood swings, depression, and reckless activities are just a few examples of what you are highly susceptible to during this period. Your emotional scabs have yet to develop to a point where they can provide enough protection from those things on their own, which is why you must be conscious of what you do to nurse your wounds back to health.

This underscores the importance of establishing an effective self-care routine early on in your divorce. Without one, you open yourself up to external factors that could delay or prevent your wounds from healing properly. In fact, your injury could become worse.

There are a number of activities you can incorporate into this routine. Here, I'll share a comprehensive approach that focuses on your mental, physical, and spiritual well-being. Not only will these activities help you heal, but you'll also experience growth and transformation along the way as you strengthen yourself from within. I liken it to the transformation process of a caterpillar. In order to become a butterfly, it must isolate itself from harmful things, within its cocoon, and digest the non-essential parts of itself to reach new heights.

This self-care routine is all about becoming that butterfly. It requires focusing on what you can control and having faith that you can handle whatever comes your way. It involves making life adjustments, some of which may be uncomfortable or scary at times, and taking responsibility for your joy and happiness. It's spending time alone to deepen your sense of self. The more you understand and accept you for who you are, the more authentic you will be. Spiritually speaking, your internal glow will begin to shine as you head into your next phase of life. You'll naturally attract things and people into your life that match your energy and support your growth. You'll replace those nonessential parts of yourself with something needed for your transformation.

This may sound overwhelming and far-fetched right now, but with patience and consistency it will become your reality. There will be days when you have setbacks or feel like giving up because the process isn't working fast enough. You'll want to be healed and free of the turmoil associated with your divorce like yesterday. Understand that what you're experiencing is part of the journey, so stick to the routine and trust the process. Your divorce didn't happen overnight, and neither will your healing and transformation, so give yourself some grace.

Let's look at some activities you can incorporate into your self-care routine that will help you heal and move forward from your divorce. Apply this routine to your emotional wounds the same way you would a routine catered towards your physical wounds.

Post-Divorce Self-Care

It's helpful to involve yourself in activities you find valuable and which are beneficial to your overall growth. You should also incorporate some out-of-the-box activities in the process. What you'll find in the following self-care routine will help you do just that, while helping you grow mentally, physically, and spiritually. You will discover and rediscover things about yourself as you move forward in life, which can lead to joy and fulfillment. This will also help you make better decisions when it comes to matters of the heart.

Start your post-divorce self-care routine by creating a protective layer. Avoid as much negativity as possible. Filter out negative people, social media, TV shows and music, the news, and anyone or anything with the potential to add more pain and suffering to your wounds. That's the last thing you need right now. It's counterproductive to your healing and growth. If you can't avoid those things altogether, then limit your interactions with them as much as possible.

In addition, be selective of where you go and how you spend your time. Try to avoid environments that have sentimental value, like a favorite restaurant or vacation spot you and your ex frequently visited. These places can lead you back down memory lane and cause an emotional setback.

Surround yourself with people who support and uplift you. Spend time with people who listen and provide words of encouragement and help take your mind off what you're going through. Get into the habit of making time throughout your day to read, watch, or listen to something inspiring, motivating, or empowering. It doesn't have to be a long time, just enough to give yourself an emotional boost. I recommend doing this when you first wake up to help set your mood for the day, right before bed when you're relaxed and able to absorb the information while you sleep, and a time or two in between when you're having setbacks or just need an emotional boost.

A Mindfulness Practice

Mindfulness is a state of active, open attention to the present moment rather than the past or future. It's a form of meditation that involves an awareness of thoughts and feelings without judging them as good or bad. This is slightly different from the mindlessness exercise you practiced earlier, which avoided thoughts as you focused on your senses.

There are two key components of mindfulness: awareness and acceptance. Awareness is the knowledge and ability to focus attention on what's going on within yourself, and acceptance is the ability to observe and accept, rather than judge or avoid, your thoughts.

Practice mindfulness by observing your thoughts and emotions and exploring why specific ideas might be resurfacing. Start by finding a comfortable position to sit in and taking some deep breaths. Focus on your breathing and the sensations of the present moment, such as what you hear, smell, and feel, and the air passing in and out of your body. Close your eyes if that helps.

Now, direct your attention to the thoughts and emotions you're experiencing. What are you telling yourself? What's replaying in your mind? Sit with those thoughts without judgment or criticism. Just allow them to be as they are. In some cases, they may evoke a strong emotional reaction. Use that as an opportunity to address or resolve certain challenges in your life and gain a deeper awareness of self.

Mindfulness can be used to avoid self-criticism and judgment while identifying and managing negative emotions. It's mental therapy that provides many benefits, including lowering stress levels and helping protect you against depression and anxiety.

Explore the New

Change is one of the challenges divorce brings with it. When you've been married for a period of time, there are customs and routines you get used to. You create certain habits through regular interactions and activities with your partner. This makes you feel safe and comfortable because a part of your life is familiar and somewhat predictable.

When that routine is broken, however, as in the case of a divorce, it adds to any uncertainty about life that you may have already had. What you once imagined for your future has suddenly shifted, and now you're not sure what to expect. This can lead to a paralyzing fear.

Exploring new interests and activities will help you break free from that fear, and it can do wonders for your overall growth as an individual. It can help build your confidence and self-esteem, expose you to new ideas and new ways of thinking, connect you with like-minded people, and uncover new passions, all while you become more self-aware. Those are just some of the things I discovered during my divorce, ones that I continue to benefit from to this day.

Find something you've been curious to try, do more of, or learn about, but which you've never gotten around to. For me, it was international travel. Maybe you've always longed to explore one of the martial arts, learn a foreign language, or take up oil painting. Perhaps you're interested in a deeper study of your faith or you've always wanted to run a marathon. If the activity requires significant planning, do the necessary work and see it through.

A healing wound brings with it a natural level of discomfort. Healing is rarely a comfortable place to be. Engaging in new experiences often requires you to step outside of your comfort zone as well. This will be a challenge if fear is your constant companion, but you can overcome that fear.

There are two things I want you to be aware of when it comes to trying something new. First, it's important for you to keep an open mind. We tend to be heavily influenced by our past, so preconceived notions can keep you from stepping outside of your comfort zone. It's easy to decide not to try something new or to judge new activities unfairly based on someone else's experience or opinion, especially if that someone was an influential figure in your life as you were growing up, such as a parent or caregiver. This can stunt your growth as an individual, keeping you from experiencing life in a way that was designed for you. Maybe you'll like the experience, or maybe you won't. Either way, you'll learn something from it, while deepening your sense of self.

Second, be aware that fear is what keeps most people on the sidelines when it comes to trying something new. They're afraid to step outside of their comfort zone, which impacts their growth. Fear is one of the biggest hurdles my clients face when it comes to change, not just from a divorce, but life in general. Some fear is instinctual and healthy and keeps you alert to trouble. If it holds you back from personal growth, however, it can be destructive. If fear is common for you, there's a great book you can read called *Feel the Fear and Do It Anyway*, by Susan Jeffers. In the book, you'll find tips on how to overcome your fears, including strategies you can incorporate in your everyday life.

A lot of what you experience as fear is separate from true and immediate danger. It comes as a result of you being in the present moment while your mind is in the future trying to predict what will happen. This is what causes worry, anxiety, and nervousness. There is also an element of fear that comes from experience. If you tried something before that did not work out, you often hold on to that memory. Maybe it was something you saw someone else try unsuccessfully, and you're using that to predict your future odds of success. Your mental commentary may say something like, "What if I try this again and it doesn't work out, just like last time?" Your mind comes up with a bunch of what-ifs. You begin to look at reality through the narrative your mind has created.

With fear, the narrative is trying to convince you that the result will be something negative or unfavorable or will fail to meet your expectations. It is like watching the previews of a movie and trying to predict the ending without enough information about the plot. The more you feed into that narrative, the more fearful you will become. You then begin to come up with excuses, disguised as legitimate reasons, which support the story in your head. You may even have visions that play out in your mind. And ultimately the undesirable result your mind is showing you might be true. But so might the opposite.

The next time you find yourself paralyzed by fear, identify the reason why. Do you know with absolute certainty that your fearful thoughts will happen, or is a more favorable outcome also possible? If there are two possible outcomes, then something is causing you to lean more towards the negative one. What is that something?

Develop more faith in your ability to handle whatever comes your way. There is an inverse relationship between faith and fear. As your faith strengthens, your fear diminishes. The more you can overcome your fears, the stronger your faith will become in your ability to do so. Every time you try something new, you may still experience some level of initial fear. That fear, however, will not keep you from moving forward.

Move Your Body

Exercise is most often recommended for its physical benefits, including stronger muscles and bones, more energy, reduced risk for certain diseases, and a longer and healthier life. What may not immediately come to mind when you think about exercise, however, are the mental and emotional benefits. In its most basic form, exercise promotes feel-good chemicals in the brain, called endorphins, which help to improve your mood and make you more relaxed. This can help fight off anxiety and depression and enhance your self-esteem.

CrossFit was more than just my inspiration for this book. It became a source of mental therapy during my divorce that I eventually adopted as a way of life.

It was a different type of exercise routine for me, one that forced me to step outside my comfort zone. It challenged my mind and body in ways that no other workout had before. I broke through mental barriers by staying consistent with my workouts, despite the pain, which strengthened my ability to break through barriers moving through my divorce. Through it, I adopted the Latin phrase mens sana in corpore sano, which means "a healthy mind in a healthy body." It serves as my reminder that the health of one is connected to that of the other.

There's also a socialization benefit that comes with exercise. By joining a gym or exercise program, you're surrounding yourself with people who share health goals similar to yours. They can help motivate you and hold you accountable, as was the case with some of the people I met doing CrossFit. They became my gym family. We laughed together, shared life stories, and sweated together as we tried to catch our breath from the workouts.

Bottom line, exercise is an essential part of your physical, mental, and psychological well-being. Some form of it should be incorporated in your self-care routine.

Helping Others Heals You

As a divorcee, you may find you have extra time on your hands, time once taken up by activities involving your ex, your marriage, or being a full-time parent. To fill that empty space, consider volunteering, which is proven to be mentally and spiritually uplifting.

I signed up to be a flag football coach for seven-to-nine-year- olds at the YMCA. My primary motivation for doing this was to be a part of something bigger than myself and make a positive impact in the lives of others. Having played football from the age of nine through college, I had a natural affinity for the sport. Not only that, this would be another way for me to spend time with my son while instilling some life lessons I'd learned growing up.

When I signed up to be a volunteer, I didn't realize how much growth and inner joy I would get from the experience. Motivating those kids to do their best, correct their mistakes rather than dwell on them, and believe in themselves reinforced the same messages in me. The more I talked about it, the more it amplified my own beliefs about what I was going through and gave me newfound energy to stay positive and keep moving forward. Not only did helping others heal me, but it also eventually led me to the coaching work I'm doing now, which I thoroughly enjoy and which allows me to give back in a similar way.

According to an article on WebMD titled, "The Mental Benefits of Volunteering," volunteering can boost your mental health. The more you do it, the happier you can become.[7] Studies have shown that people who start with lower levels of well-being may get an even more significant boost of happiness from being a part of something bigger than themselves.

Another mental benefit you can expect to experience is the "helper's high," a term used to describe the feeling you get after volunteering. This feeling can be described as a prolonged calmness, a reduction in stress, and a greater sense of self-worth. You can also experience greater satisfaction with life and its purpose, increased self-confidence, and a greater sense

---

7   WebMD Editorial Contributors, "Mental Benefits of Volunteering," WebMD.com, October 25, 2021, https://www.webmd.com/mental-health/mental-benefits-of-volunteering

of identity and belonging. Volunteering can boost your social connections, which can prevent depression and loneliness. It can even grow your professional skills and expose you to new opportunities.

Despite being fully healed today, I continue to help others grow by volunteering my time to teach financial literacy through various nonprofits and other organizations in my community. This work continues to fulfill me in a number of ways, giving me a sense of purpose in life, knowing I'm helping others who may pay it forward with people in their social circles.

Choose Growth

Adam wanted more out of life, but he couldn't quite articulate what he wanted. He came to me a couple of months before his divorce was final and told me he felt stuck and uninspired. Adam was searching for answers. The events leading up to his pending divorce had left his life in shambles, and he was ready for a change. I explained to Adam that, in order to grow, he had to learn to let go of his fears and insecurities, and step outside his comfort zone.

I walked Adam through a life-balancing exercise I use to help my coaching clients find a starting point for making changes in life. The goal of this exercise is to identify areas in your life that are out of balance and come up with ways to bring them into alignment.

You can apply this same exercise if you're looking for change and unsure how to go about it. This exercise gives you something purposeful to focus on and is part of a transformation process.

Step 1: Identify an area of your life that you want to change. Choose which one you want to start with.

- Job/career
- Spirituality

- Family
- Health
- Social life
- Finances
- Romance/Intimacy
- Community/volunteer

To help Adam do this, I had him draw a circle on a piece of paper and divide it into eight sections. The picture he drew resembled a sliced pizza, with each slice representing one of the areas mentioned above. He assigned a number between one and ten in each area, according to his current level of satisfaction in that area, one being the lowest and ten being the highest. He ranked most areas between seven and nine, but social life and romance/ intimacy were the anomalies at five and four, respectively.

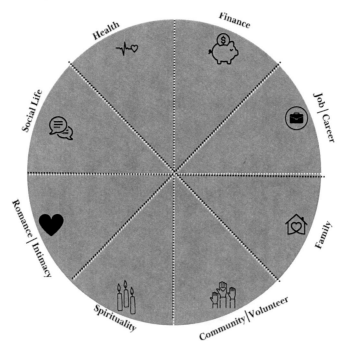

Step 2: Describe what your life is currently like in that area. Be specific. Adam wasn't having any luck connecting with women on a romantic level. Going through a divorce, it was easy for him to identify why romance/intimacy ranked low compared to the other areas. After the separation, Adam had become somewhat of a recluse. His primary reason for not hanging out or socializing as much was fear of embarrassment. A lot of the people he associated with were couples that he and his ex interacted with together.

Step 3: Identify how you got to this point in your life. Examine your habits and behaviors in these areas. What was the journey like that brought you to where you are now? What choices did you make along the way? What's keeping you there?

This was all about the divorce for Adam. In addition to feeling embarrassed, he felt awkward going out by himself. He had become accustomed to doing things with his ex. He found himself working more since the separation, which didn't leave much time for anything else. When he wasn't working, he mostly stayed to himself, doing things around the house and watching TV.

Step 4: Define what you want. Once you understand how you got here, describe what you want this area of your life to look like in the future. If it helps, close your eyes and create a visual in your mind. What do you see? How does the picture you created make you feel? Make this change real in your mind first, and feel the emotional energy associated with it. Write down your vision for the future. You can also create a vision board for this step, using images you find online or in magazines that represent what you'd like to accomplish.

Adam wanted to be social again. He had visions of traveling to different places around the world, and learning about different cultures.

Step 5: Identify the actions that will help you reach your goals. Write down all the things you will do consistently to get there. Again, be specific. If it helps, look at what's keeping you at this point in your life and do the opposite. If you decide to start traveling more, how often will you do it? Where will you go, and what will you do when you get there? Given your other priorities in life, is this a realistic plan? If not, then how can you adjust the plan to make it real?

Make sure whatever goal you set is SMART: specific, measurable, achievable, realistic, and time-bound. That's how you can measure your progress and stay on track. It's also important to identify any challenges you foresee in reaching your goal so you can properly prepare.

Remember this: people only change when they have a compelling enough reason to do so. In your mind, the benefits of doing something new have to outweigh the fear and the challenges. Otherwise, you'll fall back into old routines and habits you're most familiar and comfortable with. Write down your motivation. What's going to make it worth your time and energy to stay consistent and disciplined, despite the storms?

✱ To download your own copy
of the Choose Growth Wheel, visit
www.youwereborntoheal.com/resources. ✱

The Healing Power of Prayer

Eighty-two percent of the people I surveyed said they incorporated some form of prayer in their healing process. Most people I know pray on a regular basis, regardless of what God they pray to. It provides them with a sense of comfort and strength, while allowing them to be vulnerable without fear of judgment from the outside world. It gives people hope for a better tomorrow, and people often rely on prayer in times of pain and suffering.

I look at prayer as a way to connect spiritually with something bigger than yourself. It's your personal relationship with God and how the two of you communicate. Rooted in prayer is faith. It's not just about what you say. It's what you believe.

When the topic comes up for discussion, I share my views on prayer as a two-way street. You should listen just as much as, if not more than, you talk to God. You may be so busy telling God what you want that you don't listen for a response. We forget that "if it's in your will" part that Jesus mentions in the Bible.

Consider asking God what he wants from you in prayer. What purpose does he want you to serve, and is this the process you have to go through to fulfill it? Keep in mind that the foundation of any relationship is communication, which only works effectively when it goes both ways.

If you pray for healing, consider asking for growth and transformation as well. That way you'll know your journey is purposeful, regardless of the ups and downs, and you'll emerge a different person at the end of it. When your prayers are aligned with God's will, I believe God will open up doors and pathways to help get you there in time. That doesn't mean it will be easy or without its challenges. Have faith, focus on what you can control, and let life unfold from there.

Like many divorcees, I used prayer as a healing tool throughout my divorce process. As I moved along on my journey, I prayed for God to allow me to use my experience to help others avoid divorce altogether or grow through it if the divorce was inevitable. I felt the pain as I went through it. At the same time, I was slowly transforming into a vessel of hope and reassurance that if I can overcome the challenges of divorce, then so can others.

Your Inner Circle

Utilize family and friends, those you trust the most to have your best interest at heart, for emotional support. These are often the people who know you best and can serve multiple roles, such as a coach, sounding board, or shoulder to lean on. You should have a level of comfort talking to them without bias or fear of judgment.

If you have someone in this inner circle who's been through a divorce or serious breakup, reach out to them to see if they'd be willing to listen or share things that helped them along their journey. See if there are any similarities in your emotional experiences.

Depending on your comfort level, you might also get feedback from friends and family on your strengths and weakness. See if who you think you are aligns with the image others have of you. This will give you insight as you grow your awareness through this transition period.

> ✱ Do not allow the opinions of others to negatively influence how you feel about yourself. ✱

Journaling

Before she started journaling, Sylvia found herself thinking toxic thoughts about her ex on a consistent basis. These thoughts occupied a good portion of her day. Without an outlet, she began to slip into a state of depression.

"I kept replaying things like, 'He said this, I should've said that' in my mind, which led to depression," Sylvia said. "Journaling about those negative thoughts became therapy for me."

For Sylvia and other divorcees, journaling is a release mechanism and a form of mental therapy. In fact, according to the article titled "The Mental Health Benefits of Journaling," by

Emma Dibdin, journaling can help manage depression, anxiety, and stress, release tension and pent-up negative emotions, and enhance your self-awareness and awareness of your triggers.[8] Writing about your struggles and challenges can have a calming effect and help clear your mind of negative thoughts. I like to think about it as a detoxification for your mind, similar to what sweating does for your body.

There's something liberating about journaling when you're going through a challenging situation, like divorce. You can be as unfiltered as you want to be, about whomever or whatever, without worrying about being judged or ridiculed the way you might be if you conveyed those same thoughts and emotions out loud to someone. The toxic release benefits the mind, and I believe it benefits the spirit as well. It's like the caterpillar getting rid of the nonessential parts of itself in order to become a butterfly.

Putting those types of thoughts and emotions down on paper freed Sylvia's mind to focus on more positive things, like her value. "My self-esteem was lowered as a result of my marriage, so I had a specific journal about how I saw myself to boost my self-esteem," she said. She used journaling as a building block to get back to who she was prior to her troubled marriage, some days talking to God through her writing as well. By transferring that stored-up negative energy from thoughts to paper, she freed her cluttered mind and expanded her mental capacity to focus on something more beneficial for her overall growth.

Your story, played out on paper, will consist of deep introspection as you go back and forth with yourself as your own therapist, asking and answering questions about what happened to your marriage and how you feel about those events. As you

---

8   Emma Dibdin, "The Mental Health Benefits of Journaling," March 31, 2022, https://psychcentral. com/lib/the-health-benefits-of-journaling

spend time journaling, be sure to look back from time to time to monitor your journey. Read some of your earlier writings as a way to gauge where you are in the healing process. How has the tone of your writing changed? What has the balance between negative and positive been like? What growth opportunities are you seeing for yourself? These types of questions and self-reflection increase your awareness.

Self-esteem

Self-esteem is connected to the mental narrative you create about yourself, which is often shaped by other people's input, especially those closest to you. What they say and what you choose to believe has a lot to do with how high or low your self-esteem is. This mental image starts from early childhood and can heavily influence how you see and value yourself for the rest of your life.

Do not allow the opinions of others to negatively influence how you feel about yourself. Doing so suggests that you value their opinion about you more than your own.

✱ Not sure where you fall on the self-esteem spectrum after your divorce? Download the Self-Esteem Assessment to help. You can find out at ✱ www.youwereborntoheal.com/resources.

If you are suffering from low self-esteem as a result of your divorce, you can improve it. Identify the most common critical thoughts you have about yourself and write them down. Next to each one, write why you believe it to be true. Is it an adopted belief based on what your ex or someone else said about you? Is it self-generated through your own inner critic? Bring awareness into your why by identifying the source.

Make sure you write down something you believe to be true, something you can easily remember when you find those negative thoughts creeping back in. Repeat those affirmations every day for as long as it takes for them to sink in. Get to a point where you can recognize when those negative beliefs begin to creep in, and immediately replace them with the positive ones. Low self-esteem that is deep-rooted has tremendous momentum, so it can be a challenge for you to break away from that cycle of negative thinking. Replace what's been mentally rooted, and begin to live your life based on those affirmations until they become a part of who you are. If you have difficulty moving past these limiting beliefs on your own, seek professional help.

Another way to increase your self-esteem is to surround yourself with positive people who will uplift you. Choose to associate with people who will accept you for who you are without judgment and who already exhibit qualities of a healthy self-esteem. You can also listen to uplifting messages and stories from people you most admire.

Be mindful of who and what you are listening to and the environments you choose to be in. Negativity in the media and on social media can be very influential. Listen to people who inspire you to grow and allow your internal light to glow. Seek out people who have experienced divorce. Find out what their journey was like. There is a good chance that their self-esteem and confidence took a hit, so ask them how they were able to regroup and move forward.

> **//** These thoughts of low self-esteem have become a part of who you are, whether you realize it or not. Not only do they influence how you feel, but you're most likely projecting them in your social behaviors and interactions. Other people have come to know you for those behaviors and can feed those thoughts with similar energy through their words and actions, whether intentional or not. This helps to keep the cycle going. Transform each critical thought into a positive affirmation. **//**

Find Your Ikigai

While sitting at my desk checking email one day, the word ikigai popped into my inbox. It was the Dictionary.com word of the day, defined as "One's reason for being, which in principle is the convergence of one's personal passions, beliefs, values, and vocation." The definition resonated with me, so much so that I ordered a book about it hours later entitled, *Ikigai: The Japanese Secret to a Long and Happy Life*, by Héctor García and Francesc Miralles.

It's funny how life works sometimes. My mom had just transitioned three weeks earlier, so I was still dealing with the pain and uncertainty associated with her death. A couple of days before her funeral, my cousin Raelena came over to my parent's house to check on me and help gather some of her belongings. The two of them had enjoyed a close relationship and wore the same size, so I invited her to take any of my mom's clothes that she wanted.

As Raelena and I were talking, she mentioned a book she had read. She described it as a guide to "living your best life" but she couldn't remember the name of the book or much detail beyond that. I didn't think much more about that conversation until I posted on my Instagram account the cover of the ikigai book I had bought. A few minutes later, Raelena called to say that was the book she was telling me about at my parent's house. Chills ran through my body when she said that.

Iki, meaning life, and gai, meaning value, is a Japanese word that can be interpreted as the values in your life that make it worth living.[9] It's also been described as your reason for being; that which gets you out of bed in the morning, and drives you to share the best of yourself with others; finding joy and fulfillment

---

9   Yukari Mitsuhashi, *Ikigai: Giving Every Day Meaning and Joy*, (Kyle Books, 2018).

in life by living on purpose.

Each person's ikigai is different and can change over time, but finding it ultimately boils down to self-awareness. Knowing what you want and value in life is key to discovering your ikigai. Maybe it comes in the form of dancing, cooking, gardening, volunteering, writing, traveling, exercising, or a combination of those activities. Your ikigai is not specific to one thing, but rather a part of your lifestyle. One of the core principles of ikigai is focusing on individual moments, not just the big picture of life. In that way it's closely aligned to being present, and giving meaning and joy to everyday living.

For many people, knowing their ikigai can help them find a stable state of mind, feel more driven and motivated, grow and progress, find a sense of purpose and vitality to live and move forward, become more proactive, and feel happy and content.[10]

10   Yukari Mitsuhashi, *Ikigai: Giving Every Day Meaning and Joy*, (Kyle Books, 2018).

This can be beneficial when dealing with uncertainty about where your life is headed after divorce, when you might struggle to find something to help keep you grounded and motivated. It can help you identify what's truly important in life and where to place your focus and energy while going through your relationship transition.

My client Renée found her ikigai in designing swimsuits and socializing. She was transitioning out of a three-year relationship with a man she had fallen deeply in love with, and she was looking for solace. In an effort to help her move forward, I asked her to reflect back over her life and tell me about the times she felt the most joy and happiness. I wanted to know her motivations, and when she felt a sense of purpose and fulfillment. Turns out she'd been a fairly social person from a young age, who enjoyed meeting and learning about people. She was also creative, having received a number of awards for art, poetry, and creating plays in school. One of her favorite things to do as a child was sewing outfits for her Barbie dolls. Whenever she was feeling down, those were the things that made her feel better.

I encouraged her to get back into similar activities during this transition period. Placing her focus and energy into these activities would help take her mind off what she was going through. She did just that, and has since started a business designing swimwear for women. She also joined a social club of like-minded people who give back to the community. The two activities brought a sense of joy and fulfillment to her life, giving her a sense of purpose. Tapping into her ikigai helped Renée heal and grow.

Your ikigai can also be associated with your work. Those who find their ikigai through work have a passion for what they do and get paid for it. You won't think about "work" in a negative sense, such as something you have to or are forced to do, but rather something you want to do because you enjoy doing it and it fulfills a purpose bigger than yourself. Your ability to do this type of work often comes naturally, and is improved with time and effort.

Finding your ikigai happens at the convergence of four questions:

- What do you love to do?
- What are you good at?
- What does the world need?
- What can you be paid for?

At the intersection of your answers to these questions is your work ikigai.

I've given you a general sense of what Ikigai is, the lifestyle associated with it, and how it can help you find joy and fulfillment in life during your divorce. Take time to find your ikigai in everyday activities as you heal and progress towards a new way of living. There are a number of books and information online that go into more detail if you'd like to learn more about it.

Be in Partnership with Time

Know that in time you will heal from this experience. Focus on the system you put in place to do so rather than on the end goal. Regularly engage in activities that bring you peace, happiness and purpose, and which provide a healthy outlet mentally, physically, and spiritually. Maybe it's traveling, teaching a class or coaching, picking up a new hobby, starting a new workout routine, or pursuing a passion.

Whatever you decide to do, create a routine that incorporates these activities. Your attitude and behavior will begin to change as your emotional scabs grow and eventually fall off. Things that used to bother you won't be as impactful anymore, if at all.

Over time, you'll be in partnership with what's natural as you heal those wounds.

This is not a microwave or quick-fix experience, but one that requires patience and a commitment on your part to nurture your divorce wounds back to health. This is about small gains and getting better each day, so trust the process. Setbacks are a part of the journey, so give yourself some grace when they happen. As with life itself, this experience won't be without its share of challenges. Embrace these challenges and use them to focus on your personal growth.

Mistakes to Avoid

When I re-injured my hand by using it too soon, I had to relive some painful parts of that experience. Not only that, I also had to restart parts of my self-care process that I'd already moved past. I was already missing the gym, and this new injury further delayed my return.

Reentering the dating game too soon without healing or knowing what you want in another person can lead to a rebound relationship. These types of relationships are based on reactions to a previous relationship and the issues you might still be dealing with from the breakup. Your emotional experience from a divorce can create an ideal setting for wanting a new relationship to heal your wounds.

It's not uncommon to want to jump into another relationship soon after a divorce or even before the divorce is finalized. Loneliness is a major reason for this rush. You may have a longing to be with someone who meets your desires, mentally or physically, simply because that's what you're accustomed to. You miss having a warm body lying next to you at night or someone to talk to and hang out with. Another reason you might be tempted to jump into a new relationship is to get back at your ex. You want to prove to them that you can thrive on your own. You want to show them you can connect with someone else despite what they may have said about your ability to do so. You may also have concerns that your friends and family members will distance themselves from you or no longer invite you to certain events because you are single.

The mind can create a variety of different scenarios that make rebound relationships look appealing. They may feel right at first, but if you're not careful you can find yourself frustrated, disheartened, and even confused. You may lose confidence in your ability to love again or to make sound decisions in who you choose as a partner. Your self-esteem can take a hit, and the attitude you have about the opposite sex may become negative. These things have the potential to set you back in an area of your life that was already fragile.

If the person you are dating gets emotionally attached, you also run the risk of hurting them in the process. This can damage their view of relationships. One of my clients, Rah, shared with me how bad he felt for jumping into another relationship shortly after separating from his wife. He told the woman he was dating that, even though his divorce wasn't final, he didn't have feelings for his wife anymore and was ready to move on. The marriage had been unofficially over long before the separation. After a few months of dating her, he began to realize that wasn't completely true. By this time, the woman he was dating had become emotionally attached, and was devastated when he said that he and his estranged wife were going to try and work things out.

Be mindful of who you involve yourself with romantically during this time and where your heart is. Process your emotions until your reasons for dating are no longer tied to your previous partner. Before jumping into a new relationship, understand your motives behind the decision and the impact your actions may have on you and your new partner. Are you motivated by selfish desires that have more to do with your divorce than with a genuine connection to someone long-term? Any reasons involving your ex can indicate you're not ready because you haven't let go of the hurt and pain.

Look out for these traits of rebound relationships:

- You often compare your current relationship to your previous relationship.
- You don't give your new relationship your full attention. You're just going through the motions.
- You're more confused about what a relationship should be than you were when you were married.
- You jumped into another relationship to get over your previous relationship.
- You're not accustomed to being alone, so you jump into another relationship to fill a void.
- You feel like you have something to prove to your ex or other people.

At the minimum, be transparent with whomever you find yourself becoming attached to. Before emotions get too involved on either side, have a conversation with them about where you are on your journey and what emotions you're still dealing with. Give them a choice as to whether they want to stay or leave to reduce the risk of emotional backlash, on both parts.

Chapter 4.

The Scar: An Insightful Reminder

Many scars fade over time and become invisible to the eye, but never completely go away. You learn to live with them, until one day they become an afterthought. Although you can heal from your divorce, you will never completely forget it. Some portion of that experience will remain with you forever. Don't be alarmed or worried, however. Those memories are not meant to hold you hostage to your past, but rather to help you move forward from it with more awareness. They can keep you from repeating the same mistakes. I refer to this final phase of the healing process as the emotional scar.

These scars represent the lessons learned from your divorce. Much like physical scars, emotional scars are a natural part of the healing process. They serve as a reminder of what you've been through to get to this point in your life. The highs and lows, the challenges, the disruption. It's an experience you'd rather not repeat if you can help it. You now have more awareness of what went right and wrong and who you are as a person, so it's up to you to apply that knowledge moving forward.

One of my scars after my divorce was the reality of my son not growing up in a two-parent household. I wanted him to experience something I had not—both biological parents living under the same roof, raising him to the best of their ability. I knew what the statistics said, and I'd heard the stereotypes about Black men as fathers. I was determined to do things differently. More importantly, I wanted to have a daily connection with my son and influence his life in a positive direction.

My desire to have daily interaction with my son also came from the fact that I had become the product of a broken household when my mom and biological dad, who never married, went their separate ways. They split up when I was about two, around the same age my son was when his mom and I separated. I did not want to repeat the cycle.

My mom often said my biological dad did a lot for me when I was younger. I spent every summer with him and my great-grandma in the country. He would make the twenty-five minute drive from Woodstown, New Jersey, to Wilmington, Delaware, once school was out, and take me back with him. When it was time to go back to school, he would pack up my things and return me to Wilmington.

My dad took me to places like Wildwood, New Jersey, and the Saturday night rodeo at Cowtown. He taught me how to ride my first bike, telling me to "get up" and "stop crying" when I veered off the road and into the ditch. He bought me a go-kart that I rode in the grass around the house, around and around, until it ran out of gas. Those are the good times I still remember.

As I got into my middle school years, my dad became more

distant and uninvolved. If I wanted to go visit him and my great-grandma, my mom would have to take me and pick me up. When I was there, I barely saw him, and I don't remember much in the way of meaningful conversation. I'm sure we still did things, but unfortunately, nothing stands out in my memory.

By the time I reached high school, I barely saw or heard from him. My dad never came to any of my football games or track meets or anything else I did in school or elsewhere. This wasn't because he wasn't allowed to or did not have the means to. He just chose not to. For whatever reason, other things became more important to him.

His absence during my formative teenage years created a rift between us that was never fully repaired before he died, which, despite having a stepfather in the house, left a void in my life. I sought validation, guidance, and identity. What role did my father play in some of my thought processes and actions? What was his life like growing up? So many things went unsaid.

Fortunately, my stepfather stepped in and did his best to give me guidance. He showed up as an active father for me. It wasn't until I was in college that my aunt told me the story of my dad's relationship with his biological father. Apparently it was worse than the one he and I had, as his biological father had never been a part of his life. Unfortunately, I never got a chance to talk to my dad about his relationship with his father. I never had the opportunity to understand how he had been affected by that relationship or how it may have impacted our relationship as I got older. He died when I was in my mid-twenties.

I was determined not to repeat with my son the cycle that had already affected at least three generations. I was fortunate to have an ex who wanted me to be just as much a part of his life as she was, so we had no issues when it came to co-parenting. We worked out a custody schedule and stuck to it for the most part. She understood what I had experienced with my biological father, and she didn't want our son to experience the same thing.

As a result of my childhood scar, I remain active in my son's life today. I remembered feeling abandoned and rejected by my dad, and I didn't want my son to ever experience those feelings in our relationship. I coached his tackle and flag football teams and ran an All-Pro Dad program at his elementary school when he was younger. I took him on trips to the beach, professional football and basketball games, and wrestling matches as he got older. The scar has helped me to break the cycle.

As my story illustrates, scars may be painful to get, but you can use them to remind you to do things in a way that works better for you in the future. By the time you reach this phase of your divorce process, you've wrestled with a lot of emotions along your journey. Hopefully, you've come to terms with your divorce and have accepted it as another chapter in your life. This acceptance has created a peace within, and you can now start your next chapter. If you can make it through this, then you can make it through anything. Few events in life rival the mental and emotional impacts of a divorce.

If you've done the work along the way, you're more confident by the time you reach this point because you've stepped outside of your comfort zone and tried things you haven't before. You now know what it takes to heal. The journey has taught you some new things about yourself and allowed you to adjust some old ways of thinking and behaving. You've deepened your awareness of your experiences and your reactions to them. As a result, you now have a greater sense of what it takes for you to have joy and happiness.

Divorce is just another part of life that comes with its share of ups and downs. Having gone through those ups and downs, having made it through one after another and another, you realize you have the ability to not only bounce back from whatever challenges you face, but to also do so in a way that makes you even stronger. You've become more resilient as a result. Life gives you all kinds of reminders of your past. Pictures, videos, and even your children can remind you of who you once were. Physical and emotional scars that remain after the healing is done can remind you, too.

Some people see emotional scars as a bad thing, and they can be. You can be so scarred that you won't allow yourself to open your heart again, to give love and romance another chance. You can allow your past to paralyze your present in that area of your life.

I look at scars in a different way. I didn't stop doing pull-ups once my hand was healed. I made it a point to wear gloves, instead, to help reduce the risk of re-injury. In the same way, emotional scars allow you to be wiser and set healthy boundaries. You allow people into your life who have the right credentials, much like a security guard who checks IDs before allowing people into a building. They understand the potential ramifications of allowing people in who don't belong there. You can't just tell them you belong in the building; you have to show them as well. Your scars allow you to recognize those credentials based on the values, boundaries, beliefs, and characteristics you've defined and redefined through self-awareness and experience. Rather than paralyze you, your scars make you more conscious of the steps you need to take in order to move forward in the right direction.

Signs You Are Healed

How long does it take to heal from divorce? Whenever I get that question, my answer is always the same: It depends on the person. The majority of the divorcees that I surveyed said it took them one to two years to heal. Everyone heals in their own time and way. I often compare it to the time it takes babies to walk. Some start before the age of one (me), while others start later (my son).

There are many factors involved in the healing process, such as the length of your marriage, whether you have children, and how amicable the split was. It also has a lot to do with your ability to rebound from life situations in general and the consistency and effectiveness of your self-care routine.

There are signs, however, that can indicate your progress towards being healed from your divorce. To give you a sense of where you might be on your journey, consider some of the responses I received from the survey when I asked how respondents knew they were healed.

"When I stopped asking myself if this was the right decision." – Mike M.

"I could see my ex and not feel guilty/apprehensive/nervous. Also my stress level decreased." – Tiffani W.

"When I began to have a more balanced perspective on what caused our divorce and recognized all the positive outcomes as a result of the divorce." – Allisa J.

"When I was able to forgive and move on with my life!" – Darin W.

"He wasn't the center of my thoughts. And I could go days without thinking about him or the divorce." – Althia M.

"I was able to talk about the divorce without anger or sadness." – Cynthia

"I was able to move forward and not think about the past and the deception." – Paulette G.

"I stopped worrying about bumping into her in public, was able to have arguments in my new relationship and not flashback, was able to pray for her and leave her with God, felt comfortable helping others who were going through similar situations." – Mark D.

"When dealing with situations that normally would cause a reaction, I was more mature and handled it differently." – Brandon B.

"I was ready to move on with my life and explore other relationships, and I was no longer concerned about matters that concerned my ex." – Sharlene K.

"I was able to look at the past as a valuable part of my life and had no regrets." – Jamila G.

"Being transparent about my part in the divorce. Using my errors to grow and being prepared to enter a reciprocal friendship/relationship with someone else." – Gardine W.

Can you say some of the same things? Use these responses to gauge your progress and any additional work you may need to do to arrive at a place of healing.

A good friend of mine, who I'll call John, had recently separated from his wife of ten years and was heading towards divorce. Every time John and I talked, which was about twice a month, the conversation started out the same way. We'd exchange some friendly banter, crack some jokes about each other, and talk about sports or the latest news.

In the midst of our conversations, John would always find a way to make comments about his broken marriage and soon-to-be ex-wife. It didn't matter what we were talking about. He'd find a way to spin the conversation into what he was going through. The majority of those comments were negative and directed towards his wife and what she did or didn't do that led to the demise of their marriage. His face would often tense up when he talked about it.

I figured John needed an outlet, so I'd listen to him talk,

share some of my experiences around the subject, and give some advice when asked. Every once in a while, his estranged wife would call him while we were talking, and I could hear the disdain in his voice when he answered. His responses were curt, and as soon as he hung up, he would go on a rant about something she said or wanted. This communication pattern started shortly before they got separated and went on for months after their divorce was final. Clearly, John wasn't healed yet.

I can listen to someone talk and know early on if they're still dealing with some residual negativity from their divorce. I can tell when they're still holding on to something that's manifesting itself through random, unexpected conversations. In John's case, this negativity continued for about a year after his divorce before it began to change.

When you're moving towards a place of healing, you no longer allow your past to negatively impact your present. You begin to break free from the manipulation and other forms of mental and emotional abuse you may have suffered, and you embrace your truth.

When you can see your ex and no longer get overly emotional, that's another sign that you're healing. You've accepted the divorce, even if you didn't initiate it, and you're no longer in denial or trying to make the marriage work. These signs have one major thing in common. They involve letting go of negative energy from the past, which frees up space for more positive energy to flow in for present and future living. And that's what healing is all about.

S.C.A.R.

Scars represent what you've been through. They're your life experiences and lessons learned along the way. They remind you of who you've become as a result of the wounds suffered during your divorce and the self-care routine you followed afterwards. Scars represent the last phase of the healing process. This phase will help you move forward, using a combination of what you've learned and what you've come to desire for your life.

A number of benefits can result from your scars, the important ones being growth and transformation. To remember more benefits of your scars, keep in mind the acronym S.C.A.R., which stands for secure, confident, accepting, and resilient.

S is for secure. You've become more secure in who you are as a person. You're not the same person now as you were before or during the divorce. You've healed, which means growth has taken place. Your experiences have taught you some valuable lessons and made you more self-aware. You also understand more about how to manage your emotions and transform your way of thinking.

The journey has taught you some new things about yourself and allowed you to adjust some old ways of thinking. As a result, you now have a greater sense of what it takes for you to experience joy and happiness and how you can avoid some of the negativity that plagued you along the way.

With this awareness, you can align yourself with people and things that are important to you and what you value the most without feeling guilty or obligated to be someone you're not. You no longer allow the opinions of others to influence you in a negative way. You value your opinion of yourself more than someone else's opinion of you. Being comfortable in your own skin requires a healthy self-esteem, which can take a hit as a result of a divorce, but once you've healed from your divorce, you're once again secure in yourself as a worthy and capable person.

C is for confident. You're now more confident in your ability to handle whatever may come your way. You've made it through one of the most emotional and trying experiences in life, one that's often compared with death. You know what it means to overcome challenges and push through despite the doubts, fears, and emotional setbacks. You know what it takes to heal.

Realize that life is going to happen whether you want it to or not, and there's only so much you can do to prepare for it. Develop more faith in your ability to handle whatever comes your way from here on out, and continue to grow your confidence. There will forever be an aspect of the unknown, and things that happen outside of your control. Operate within your span of control, namely your attitude and effort.

A is for accepting. Through your healing work, you've learned to accept the things that you cannot change. If there's nothing you can do to change the situation, then you accept it as if you have chosen it and move forward from there. You make decisions and choices that advance you towards your goal. There's no need to create additional pain and suffering by dwelling on what happened. You can't change it. The universe is going to unfold the way it was designed. Every choice you make will lead you to your ultimate destination, whatever that may be, with a series of unavoidable, yet purposeful, potholes along the way.

R is for resilient. There will be challenges, but you will bounce back. Divorce is just another phase in life that comes with its share of challenges. Having made it through so many of those challenges, you realize you have the ability to not only bounce back from whatever you face, but to do so in a way that strengthens you. You've become more resilient as a result.

No Guarantees

There is such a thing as being too guarded. This can be a sign that your scars have kept you from moving forward. An element of fear has come in about the future. *What might happen if he or she does the same thing as my ex? What if my heart is broken again? I don't know if I can take that.* Psychological time has taken over again, which is a sign that your scars are still fading and you're not yet fully healed.

At this point, you're oscillating between past and future, which is keeping you in fear. That inner voice is creating future negative scenarios that are based on your past, and you've bought into them. The more you associate yourself with them, the stronger they become. Before you know it—if you know it—you're caught in this mental vortex you can't seem to find your way out of. It's blocking out any other scenarios that paint a different picture than what it wants to show. It has consumed you.

If you're thinking about future possibilities, then why not think more towards the positive side? What happens if you meet someone who treats you the way you want to be treated and meets your needs? That's just as real a possibility as the one keeping you paralyzed in fear. Do you not trust yourself enough to do so? Is your faith not that strong? You do have a choice after all. Things could go either way.

I know things can get complicated when it comes to matters of the heart. When you've opened yourself up to love and been hurt before, it's not easy to recover from that. That level of pain can prevent you from being vulnerable again. That's a scar that doesn't serve you.

The reality is there are no guarantees. You could know yourself now better than ever, have learned your lessons, and think you've made the right choice this time, only to end up in another broken relationship. When you're dealing with another person there's always that possibility. It takes two people to make a relationship work, and you both have to be on the same page when it comes to being in a committed relationship.

Several of my clients and people I know who've been divorced have experienced this. Despite the work they've done to heal and move forward, they've still found themselves in relationships that didn't work. In some cases this wasn't because of anything they did. It was because of the other person. In some cases that person just wasn't ready, or maybe they were dealing with their own fears and insecurities. Manipulation and other selfish desires also come into play. Oftentimes these things don't reveal themselves in the relationship right away, and you can spend valuable time walking down a path opposite of what you had hoped for.

I've reinforced the message to them that God, the universe, is not going to align you with just anybody. And nor should He. You're unique by design, setup for greatness, so the relationship worked out the way it was supposed to. Consider this a blessing in disguise. Accept it as such, take the lessons learned, and move forward from there. If you need to revisit the self-care routine from your divorce, then by all means do so. Take whatever time you need to heal. Just don't give up on love. Your story is still being written.

Chapter 5.

Preparing for Love Again

When it's time to prepare for another phase in life—one that includes dating again and entering a new relationship—I want you to be well equipped with tools that will help increase your chances of success. In some ways, your divorce experience has prepared you for your future relationships. With the lessons learned along the way and the introspection you've done, you have a heightened self-awareness about who you are and what you need when it comes to matters of the heart.

Assuming you've reached a point where you're ready to move on, a new relationship can bring with it a renewed sense of hope and purpose, adding value to your life in a number of ways. Aligning with the right person can strengthen your self-esteem and confidence. You have the opportunity to start fresh with more wisdom. The key is applying it.

There are two primary reasons for dating: just for fun or

for something more permanent. The two can be exclusive of each other, or "just for fun" can lead to something deeper and more connected. I'm going to focus this chapter more on the latter. When you're ready to open yourself up to love again, when you've done the necessary work within yourself, there are some things you can do that will lead you to a more favorable relationship outcome than your marriage had.

While there are no guarantees your next relationship will work out the way you want it to, these things can help set you up for success. You can help shape your future by preparing for it rather than trying to predict or control it. Let's look at an effective way of doing that.

Dating After Divorce

When I first started dating again, I was so used to being in a committed relationship that I wanted to be in another one right away. My body yearned for the physical pleasures that came along with my marriage, and my mind enjoyed the sense of security, stability, and creature comforts. My ex-wife and I had dated and been married for almost a decade, so it was what I knew and was familiar with. As a result, I convinced myself I was ready to date again, but in reality, I wasn't.

At that point in my life, I hadn't spent enough time healing from the divorce and preparing myself for a healthy, successful relationship. Most of the women I dated afterwards picked up on that, and only allowed themselves to get so close to me. One of them flat-out told me, after several weeks of dating, that I wasn't ready for anything serious, despite me saying otherwise.

What led her to say that? I was still dealing with some residual negativity towards my ex, and I talked about it often. I'd somehow find ways to tie general conversations that had nothing to do with her or my marriage, back to her and my marriage. I didn't realize it at the time, but that was a telltale sign that I was still healing and not ready to jump into another committed relationship.

In another case, my new partner and I invested a lot of time together, only for the relationship to end with us going our separate ways. That experience became an important life lesson for both of us, which we eventually grew from and moved on from. That's when I realized I had to make a change to avoid perpetuating the problem.

I learned a lot of things from my dating experiences after the divorce, but there are two in particular that stand out, which I share with my clients as they are looking to date again. Both are of equal importance.

The first lesson is to be honest with where you are in life and what you want. If you're not ready to be in a committed relationship yet, let the person you're dating know that. If you're more interested in something physical right now, you just want someone to talk to, or you're looking for someone to hang out with from time to time, then communicate that. If you're not sure what you want, you need to share that too. By doing so, you let the person know your intentions and where you stand upfront, and you give them the power to choose how involved they want to be with you from there. Withholding that information for malicious intent is not fair to the other person. Avoid feeding into your selfish desires at the emotional expense of others.

When you're dating someone new, they may ask questions about your intentions early on, maybe after one or two dates. If they do, you don't have to tell them all the details about your divorce or what you're going through. It's okay to say, "I'm still dealing with some things from a previous relationship, and not ready for anything serious right now." It's your truth and lets the other person know where you are mentally.

If they don't ask, then at some point you have to bring it up. If not within the first couple of dates, then whenever you start to feel a connection, or sense that they do, initiate the discussion. Again, speak your truth. You can lead off with something like, "I've enjoyed our time together, but I want you to understand my situation and thoughts about dating right now." Whether or not the person likes what you say, they'll have to respect your honesty. You're giving them a relationship choice to make based on where they are and what they want.

Just make sure your words and actions are aligned. Avoid giving off mixed signals. In other words, if you're not ready for a serious relationship, then watch how much time and energy you give that person if they choose to stick around. Doing relationship-type things that create an emotional and physical connection may be misinterpreted. This can lead to unintentional consequences that can hurt you and the other person down the road.

The second lesson is to make sure you have spent the necessary time preparing yourself for a healthy relationship before jumping into dating seriously again. This will require an honest self- assessment of who you are in life and in love. Things have changed since you got married, especially if you've been married for a while. You've had different experiences since your earlier dating years, so you're not the same person. Your priorities may have shifted. What you want out of life and love may no longer be the same. This preparation process is pivotal.

Prepare for a Successful Relationship

The success of your next relationship depends on two factors— you and your partner. Your abilities to fulfill each other's needs, adapt to change, and weather the storms have a lot to do with it.

The two of you must share similar goals and values, like where you want the relationship to go and what your spiritual beliefs are. You don't have to agree on everything, but it helps to respect the other person's opinion. Listen for understanding, not judgment or criticism. You come from different backgrounds and have different experiences. The foundation of your relationship is effective communication.

Let's continue to focus on that one and only thing you can control—you.

Prepare for a successful relationship the same way you might prepare for a major test, sporting event, presentation, or job interview. Instead of studying information, however, study yourself. What are your interests and values? What's your love language and your attachment style? What's your happy place, and what are your deal breakers? Answer questions about yourself that you would want to know about someone else before dating them.

You're a different person coming out of your marriage than you were going into it, so learn everything there is to know about who you are and what you value now. In addition, examine what you believe to be true about yourself and why. Who or what influenced those beliefs, and why do you subscribe to them? Look back over the choices you've made to get to this point in life. Knowing what you know now, what might you have done differently?

The more time and effort you put into this awareness exercise, the more you immerse yourself in learning about yourself, the more solid your personal foundation will be. Knowing and accepting who you are without judgment or criticism will strengthen your self-esteem and confidence. This will help you identify people you're most compatible with, which will increase your chances of being in a healthy, successful relationship.

A foundational ingredient for a successful relationship is self-awareness. Without it, you're more likely to find yourself with someone you're incompatible with or to put up with situations that you shouldn't. The following actions will help you create that awareness and establish some guiding principles for dating and successful relationships.

Define the type of relationship you want. Do you want to be in a committed relationship that eventually leads to marriage? Are you looking for something more casual, like a companion? Maybe you just want to let things grow organically and see what happens from there. Clearly define what you are looking for in a relationship at this point in your life, and then ask yourself why. What benefit would this type of relationship bring into your life? What's motivating you to want to be in this type of relationship? Getting clear on these things will help you stay focused and avoid wasting time with people who are not on the same page.

List some characteristics of your ideal partner. Include the mental, physical, and spiritual traits you're looking for in that person. Then, rank them in order of importance. Compare that list to what you had in your marriage and previous relationships. Look for any patterns. Is there anything you need to modify or prioritize differently?

Do you exhibit some of those same characteristics you desire in a partner? If you want someone who is honest and trustworthy, for example, are you those things as well? It's unfair to expect your partner to be one way when you don't meet your own standard.

In addition to examing their characteristics, ask yourself questions like, what are some of their interests? What do you see the two of you having fun doing together? In what ways could they help balance you? Not that the two of you have to like all the same things or have the exact same definition of fun, but it helps to have some things in common. These types of questions will help align you with someone who shares similar interests and values.

Examine yourself for any residual negativity from your divorce or past relationships. Be honest with yourself. This might dig up some old wounds that generate strong emotions, but it's important to identify what's still keeping the negativity alive. What steps are you taking to move past it?

Letting go of what someone did to hurt or offend you releases their control over you. Cutting the cord that connects you to that person allows you to move forward with less baggage and negativity. If you can't do that on your own, then consider seeking professional support. This isn't to say that you can't date with some lingering negativity. If you choose to do so, however, consider sharing your struggle with the person you're dating when things become more emotional between the two of you. Maybe that person will be willing to help you overcome it.

A friend of mine found himself in that exact situation. The woman he was dating was insecure, constantly checking up on his whereabouts and restricting some of his movements, not because of anything that he did to break her trust. Turned out she had been cheated on in the past, and she had yet to resolve it fully. They talked it over, and he chose to help her through it. A year later they got married.

Identify qualities you have that would be beneficial to a relationship. A relationship should benefit both parties. You'll need each other's support in various ways as you grow and develop the relationship. Use the following checklist to identify some of those qualities by choosing all that apply.

☐ I am accepting of my partner, their good and their bad.

☐ I can forgive my partner when they make a mistake, let

me down, or hurt me.

☐ When I make a mistake, let my partner down, or hurt them, I quickly make amends.

☐ I am open and honest about my thoughts, feelings, and beliefs.

☐ I understand we must nurture our relationship in order for it to grow and develop.

☐ I do not keep score or try to get even in my relationship.

☐ I accept and honor our differences, realizing we are two unique individuals.

☐ I know I am responsible for meeting my own emotional needs.

☐ I am nonviolent and take responsibility for my emotions.

☐ I take responsibility for my own behavior without blaming or justifying.

☐ When we disagree, I am willing to listen to my partner's perspective without judgment.

☐ I do not engage in name-calling, put-downs, humiliation, coercion, manipulation, or domination.

☐ I do not withhold affection, sex, or attention to punish or manipulate my partner.

☐ When I am having a bad day, I let my partner know so they will understand my mood.

☐ I do not threaten to end our relationship when we have disagreements.

☐ I understand we both need to have healthy friendships outside the relationship.

☐ I have other people to talk to so I do not rely solely on my partner.

☐ If I feel jealous, I can talk to my partner about my concerns.

- [ ] I am secure in my role in our relationship for the most part.
- [ ] I look for points of agreement when we have conflict.
- [ ] I am willing to give and take so we can both win in a negotiation.
- [ ] I turn toward my partner, not away from them, when we are under stress.
- [ ] I strive for more positive interactions in our relationship.
- [ ] I know what my partner needs from me to feel loved and understood.
- [ ] I like to have fun with my partner and enjoy quality time together.
- [ ] I am honest about my concerns when they arise.
- [ ] I enjoy time alone.

If there's anything else you want to add to this list, write it down. I encourage you to also explore the traits you don't have and determine whether they were problematic in previous relationships. If you find that some of these qualities remain, you now have something to consider changing as you prepare for another relationship.

For example, maybe you want to be more open and honest about your thoughts, feelings, and beliefs, but you've been silenced, judged, or ridiculed in the past for doing so. As a result, you keep these things to yourself. Doing this has led to poor communication in past relationships, and you want to break that cycle. What can you do to change this going forward?

Keep your partner's needs in mind. Understand what they are, and actively work to fulfill them. If your partner needs words of affirmation, be sure to incorporate that into your relationship. If it's quality time, understand what that means for them and commit yourself to doing it. It's easy to get into a habit or routine as time passes, so check in periodically to make sure their needs are being met.

Listen for understanding. As your partner expresses themselves, relinquish your judgments and interpretations, and listen to understand where they're coming from. Repeat, in your own words, the message you heard, and get confirmation that you're correct. Understanding the reasons behind what they say and putting yourself in their shoes will help put things in context and make for better communication. You'll begin to understand them in a different way, one that's much deeper.

Support their ideas. Do this with words and actions. Be a sounding board to help flesh out these ideas, or give them additional things to consider. If you don't agree with their idea or it seems unrealistic (like a fifty-year-old former high school football star who wants to try out for the NFL), don't be overly critical or judgmental. Suggest alternatives instead.

Do activities they enjoy doing. This is a way to show your support and that you care about them. Even if you're not a fan of what they enjoy doing, make it a point to get engaged. I'm sure there are aspects of your job that you don't enjoy, but you do them anyway because you know it must get done. Treat these activities in much the same way, minus the negative emotions.

The Importance of Boundaries

Before you go into your next relationship, clarify your relationship boundaries. They'll help you keep yourself and your values safe, stop people from walking all over you, and help you distinguish between what you consider to be right and wrong. Without boundaries, you might put up with situations that conflict with who you are as a person.

By setting boundaries, you're not trying to control anyone. Instead, you're saying, "You can do that, but there will be consequences." If you feel guilty about setting boundaries, shift your perception of the purpose of boundaries. They're not a punishment or something negative to use against other people. It's all about you and protecting yourself.

To set boundaries, you must first be clear on the behaviors that bother you. Maybe you don't like to be ignored. You consider going days at a time without hearing from someone you're in a relationship with inconsiderate and disrespectful. Once you clarify what bothers you, set your boundaries based on those unwanted behaviors and communicate them early on.

Finally, and most importantly, you must enforce the boundaries you set. If you continue to be ignored, what will happen? Will you make yourself unavailable for a period of time? Will you end the relationship? Whatever you decide to do, you must stick to it. This is not an easy thing to do for a lot of people. They may threaten a certain consequence, but not execute on it. That sends a message to the other person that it's okay to keep doing what they're doing. When it comes to enforcing boundaries, follow-through and consistency are key.

Take time to write down your boundaries. Next to each one, write some possible consequences you'll enact if they're not respected.

> ✳ For a "Creating Relationship Boundaries Worksheet," visit www.youwereborntoheal.com/resources. ✳

Matters of the Heart

What are those drivers that connect you with someone on a deeper level? Whether it's something innate or developed over time, understanding that information about yourself will serve as your dating compatibility guide when you've reached that point in your life again. Two of the drivers I encourage you to explore are your love language and your attachment style. A lot of research has gone into both of these to help explain who you are in love, intimacy, and romantic relationships. They address your needs and how you relate to other people. If your needs aren't being met, you'll be able to communicate that from a place of stronger awareness.

Understand your love languages and ways in which they are fulfilled. If you're not familiar with Gary Chapman's five love languages from his book by the same name, here's a brief description of each one, along with some examples. After reading through them, identify which one best describes what you need to feel loved, which ones are most important to you, and how you like to experience them.

Although one may be primary, it's very common for people to have multiple love languages. We all need to experience love in various ways, depending on our mood and the situation. These languages often complement each other, as would be the case for someone who enjoys watching TV while lying next to their partner (quality time) and touching them in some way (physical touch).[11]

---

11 Gary Chapman, *The Five Love Languages*, (Chicago: Northfield Publishing, 1992).

The Five Love Languages

Gary D. Chapman

Physical Touch

To this person, physical touch is a powerful vehicle for communicating emotional love. This includes a wide range of behaviors from tousling your partner's hair, a squeeze, a touch, a massage, holding hands, kissing, and sexual intercourse. They particularly need touch or holding at times of distress. This person feels most secure in their love when it is expressed physically.

Acts of Service

Nothing means as much to this person as giving and receiving practical support. This includes the myriad of tasks such as cooking, cleaning, walking the dog, working to provide, etc. This is an expression of love by doing.

Receiving Gifts

To this person gifts are important symbols of love. What is important is that your partner thinks of you and makes the effort to translate that into a gift. This also includes yourself and your time, being there in a caring way at significant times or when needed emotionally.

Quality Time

This person needs together time. This means having your partner's undivided attention—looking at each other and talking, or just the two of you taking a walk. This person likes to share experiences, thoughts, feelings, and desires in an uninterrupted environment. It also involves doing things together. This may include any activities such as cooking, traveling, and playing sports, as long as the focus is enjoying being together.

Words of Affirmation

This person needs acknowledgement for who they are and what they do. They draw heavily on verbal compliments, encouragement and words of appreciation such as 'Thanks for doing . . . .' 'You look good in . . . .' 'I really appreciate you doing . . . .'

Focus on those acts that fulfill your love language. If one of yours is quality time, for example, does that simply mean being in the same room with your partner, watching TV without saying much at all, or something more engaging, like conversation over dinner? Depending on your mood, it could be a combination of both.

Once you start dating again and meet someone of interest, get to know their love language as well. Do things to cater to it on a consistent basis. This shows that you care about what's important to them, not just about your own needs being met.

Another area to explore when it comes to matters of the heart is your attachment style, a phrase used to describe specific patterns of behavior in relationships. These styles reflect how you interact and relate with people in intimate relationships. They take into account your emotional responses, how comfortable and confident you feel, any fears associated with hurt and rejection, and your longing for a close connection in relationships.

According to attachment theory, first developed by psychologist Mary Ainsworth and psychiatrist John Bowlby, a person's attachment style is shaped and developed during early childhood in response to their relationships with caregivers.[12] Romantic relationships are likely to reflect these early styles because the familiarity of our childhood experiences with those closest to us can condition us to expect the same experience in relationships with romantic partners. This isn't to say that the styles between childhood and adulthood are identical, however. Your life experiences and relationships in between can also play a role in your attachment style as an adult.

The four adult attachment styles are: secure, anxious,

12 Kelly Gonsalves, "The 4 Attachment Styles In Relationships + How To Find Yours," MindBodyGreen.com, April 27, 2023, https://www.mindbodygreen.com/articles/attachment-theory-and-the-4-attachment-styles

avoidant, and fearful-avoidant. The following image gives a high-level description of each.

Secure: A secure attachment style is the healthy ideal for

Secure

Effective communication skills, high self-esteem, comfortable with autonomy and in forming close relationships with others, easy to connect with.

Anxious

Clingy, jealous, difficulty trusting others and being alone, fear of rejection, highly sensitive to criticism.

Avoidant

Value independence, hard time trusting people, avoid emotional intimacy, uncomfortable expressing feelings.

Fearful - Avoidant

Contradictory behavior, difficulty regulating emotions, characteristics of both anxious and avoidant attachment styles.

relationships. Secure individuals are not afraid of intimacy or getting close to someone, and don't worry when their partner says they need some space or time apart. They can depend on others without being totally dependent, and tend to be in committed relationships longer. Some common characteristics of people with this attachment style include easily trusting of others and their intentions, comfortable being alone, being easy to connect with and emotionally available, high self-esteem, and having effective communication skills.[13] Here are some examples of what adults with a secure attachment style might say:

- "It is relatively easy for me to become emotionally close to others."
- "I am comfortable depending on others and having others depend on me."
- "I don't worry about being alone or others not accepting me."[14]

Anxious: Also known as anxious-preoccupied, this attachment style is identified by a deep fear of abandonment or rejection. People with this style tend to be insecure about their relationships, often worrying that their partner will lose interest or leave them. As a result, they constantly seek validation and reassurance from their partner. They have a tendency to suppress their own needs in order to meet the needs of others. Some common characteristics of anxious people include difficulty being alone, needing approval from others, and having low self-esteem.[15] According to relationship counselor Katarzyna Peoples, PhD, people with anxious attachment styles often feel unworthy of love and fault themselves for challenges in their relationships.[16] Here are some examples of what adults with an anxious attachment style might say:

- I want to be completely emotionally intimate with others, but I often find that others are reluctant to get as close as I would like.
- I am uncomfortable being without close relationships, but I sometimes worry that others don't value me as

---

13 Morgan Mandriota, "Here's How To Identify Your Attachment Style," October 13, 2021, PsychCentral.com, https://psychcentral.com/health/4-attachment-styles-in-relationships

14 Dr. Linda Wagener, "What is Your Attachment Style?" Headington Institute, accessed June 24, 2023, https://www.headington-institute.org/resource/what-is-your-attachment-style/

15 Morgan Mandriota, "Here's How To Identify Your Attachment Style," October 13, 2021, PsychCentral.com, https://psychcentral.com/health/4-attachment-styles-in-relationships

16 Ibid.

much as I value them.[17]

Avoidant: Also known as dismissive-avoidant, people with this attachment style often display a fear of intimacy, commitment, or a combination of the two. They tend to avoid forming close relationships in order to keep a sense of independence and invulnerability, and are quick to push people away if they feel their autonomy is being threatened. These individuals tend not to invest in or need much emotional intimacy in relationships, and experience little distress when they end, enabling them to bounce back quicker. Some common characteristics include being uncomfortable expressing your feelings, having a hard time trusting others, and a strong belief that you don't need others in your life.[18] Here are some examples of what adults with an avoidant attachment style might say:

- "I am comfortable without close emotional relationships."
- "It is important to me to feel independent and self-sufficient."
- "I prefer not to depend on others or have others depend on me."

Fearful-avoidant: This combination of anxious and avoidant attachment styles, also known as disorganized, is where people yearn for affection, but also have a fear of getting too close to someone. Their preference is for more casual relationships, or "situationships," so they may stay in the dating stage of the relationship longer, as this feels more comfortable for them. This is not always because they want to, but is often because they're afraid of commitment, intimacy, or getting hurt.[19] They tend to

---

17   Morgan Mandriota, "Here's How To Identify Your Attachment Style," October 13, 2021, PsychCentral.com, https://psychcentral.com/health/4-attachment-styles-in-relationships..

18   Ibid.

19   Morgan Mandriota, "Here's How To Identify Your Attachment Style," October 13, 2021, PsychCentral.com, https://psychcentral.com/health/4-attachment-styles-in-relationships

be more guarded with their emotions and reluctant to share too much of who they are to protect themselves from possible hurt.

"While they desperately seek love, they also push partners away because of the fear of love," says Peoples. "They believe that they'll always be rejected, but they don't avoid emotional intimacy. They fear it, and they also consistently seek it out, only to reject it again." This style is marked by confusing and unpredictable behavior—one moment they may shower you with affection, the next be aloof. Here are some examples of what adults with a fearful-avoidant attachment style might say:

- "I am somewhat uncomfortable getting close to others."
- "I want emotionally close relationships, but I find it difficult to completely trust others, or to depend on them."
- "I sometimes worry that I will be hurt if I allow myself to become too close to other people."[20]

Which attachment style do you relate to the most? Do you see yourself in more than one? I encourage you to explore your attachment styles, not through a lens of judgment, resentment or criticism, but from a place of awareness. By better understanding the role of attachment, you can gain a greater appreciation for how your upbringing and life experiences may impact your romantic relationships and what changes, if any, you want to make.

---

20   Kelly Gonsalves, "Understanding The Fearful Avoidant Attachment Style In Relationships," MindBodyGreen. com, March 22, 2023, https://www.mindbodygreen.com/articles/how-fearful-avoidant-attachment-style-affects-your-sex-life

Chapter 6.

A New You

While scrolling through my social media feed one day, I stopped when I came to a post from Jennifer, one of my former clients. It was about staying positive while chasing dreams, healing from past trauma, and still finding time to enjoy life. I couldn't help smiling when I read it and went back to look at some of her other recent posts.

Like most people I work with, she took her divorce hard and was all over the place, mentally and emotionally, when we first started talking. She'd been married for more than twenty years, with the latter part of those years unhappy. Having grown accustomed to the role of being a wife, she was unsure of what the single life would bring, and she had her share of doubts.

Something I helped her to understand early on was that she was responsible for her own joy and happiness. Allowing other people to dictate her mental well-being was giving them too much control and keeping her in a state of bondage. By relinquishing that control and accepting her new relationship status, she would open up the door for healing and transformation.

Although you can't change the past, you can learn and grow from it to make way for a better future. This was her opportunity to hit the reset button and live life differently, only this time with more experience and awareness. What did she want her life to look like? Who did she want to become?

Her social media page answered those questions. It told a story. Compared to some of her earlier posts, there were a lot more pictures of her smiling and having fun with friends. There were videos of her dancing as if no one was watching and dressed to impress at different social events. She was traveling internationally, something she hadn't done much of while married, and there were a lot more inspirational and uplifting quotes.

Whether she realized it or not, she was not only transforming into a better version of herself, but she was also helping others who might be experiencing challenges in life do the same. She was using her experience to become an inspiration for others.

I shot her a quick message that said, "Keep living your best life." She replied, "Thanks for helping to show me how." Smiley faces and praying hands followed.

I believe everything in life happens for a reason. There's a bigger purpose behind it. You may not understand the reason or agree with it, but ultimately it will help you grow if you allow it to, much like the physical pain you endure after working out at the gym or exercising for the first time in a while. With pain, your body signals you to do something different. After a tough workout, the pain may be telling you to rest those muscles, for example. Emotional pain can serve a similar purpose by nudging you to make different decisions or to make a change within yourself, in your relationships, or in your life.

Change can be uncomfortable. It often requires you to step outside your comfort zone and into unfamiliar territory, which tends to generate fear. You may believe the change will result in a negative or unfavorable outcome and therefore cling to your old patterns of thinking and behaving. Yet change is constant, so learning to embrace it, rather than resist it, will allow growth and transformation to take place naturally.

I make this clear to my clients when they are looking to change. To resist change is to resist what comes naturally. It's trying to control things you can't control instead of accepting, learning, and moving forward from them.

Divorce is not always a bad thing. Despite what society may say or try and convince you to believe, it can be one of the best things that's ever happened to you. I used to wrestle with the whole religious thing before and after my divorce, based on the vows I made before God and what other people said. It wasn't until I heard a pastor say, "God doesn't ordain every marriage. We have free will to make choices, which don't always align to His will," that my outlook on my marriage and divorce changed.

For some people, divorce is a release from a life of negativity. It's a new beginning, an opportunity for you to hit the reset button and live life differently. You're able to discover and rediscover things about yourself that bring you joy, happiness, and a sense of fulfillment. You're now free from certain responsibilities and restrictions that may have been imposed on you, despite what you believed or wanted.

What have you been released from as a result of your divorce? What are some opportunities that you now have? How will you live your life differently?

I believe there's a path in your life (in everyone's life, really) that you're meant to follow. It will eventually get you to the place you're supposed to be, but the choices you make along the way cause you to veer off course from time to time and head down a different path. This is by design. It's where you experience life and learn lessons you may consider painful, but which ultimately serve a purpose. Those lessons aren't meant only for you. They're often meant for you to share with other people who need the lessons you've learned.

The journey only stops when you are no longer living. The process continues until you serve a purpose bigger than yourself. It's a similar concept to the story of the children of Israel, who took forty years instead of forty days to reach the promised land, and what they went through to get there.

Divorce is just one of the things you experience along your journey. Nothing living in this world stays the same, which means you're constantly evolving. You will not be the same person coming out of your divorce as you were going into it. You'll either use the experience to grow, mentally and spiritually, in a positive direction, or you'll allow negativity from the experience to create further pain and suffering, keeping you trapped in fear.

When I look back at what happened to my marriage, I realize the journey helped mold me into the person I am today. Not someone perfect or even close to it, but rather someone who has become more self-aware and learned to live and thrive with imperfections while helping others do the same.

If someone would've told me when I was going through my divorce that my ex-wife and I would be taking trips and hanging out together afterwards, I wouldn't have believed them. If they'd said I'd open myself up to love and commitment after that experience, I would've adamantly denied it. If someone would've told me I'd be unemployed because of the emotional turmoil and lack of focus divorce brought into my life, I'd have questioned their sanity. Yet here I am, fifteen years removed from marriage, writing this book to let you know that those are chapters in my book of life. I couldn't have predicted this lifestyle. And I'm better as a result of my divorce journey.

I've come a long way since my divorce was final. The journey wasn't easy, nor was it quick. I struggled emotionally, jumped into relationships prematurely, and made my share of mistakes along the way. Through it all, however, I've gained a deeper sense of self, and have used my experience as a way to connect with other divorcees who need help and guidance navigating their way through life after divorce. One day you may be called upon to do the same.

As you look to make changes in your life, to redefine who you are and what you want out of life, use the following questions as a guide:

- Who do you want to become?
- What do you want your life to look like?
- What changes are you willing to make to become that person? To live that life?
- What's your motivation for wanting to do so?

Being intentional and consistent here is key. Your attitude and actions play a critical role in becoming a new and improved version of yourself. Visualize what that person looks and acts like, and begin to live based on that vision. It will eventually become your reality.

What are some of the things you're doing? What places are you visiting? Who are you spending your time with? What makes you happy? As you answer these questions in both words and actions, they will become your new reality.

If it helps, imagine yourself as a character in a movie written, directed, and produced by you. Write down what the next scene or chapter looks like for you by answering the questions above.

What challenges might you face, and how might you overcome them? How might someone else describe your character if they watched the movie? What's your love life like? Get as detailed as you would like, and use what you've written to live that life.

Transformation involves giving up a part of your old self in order to make room for something new. It can be both exciting and scary at the same time. If you're looking to grow mentally and spiritually, I want to share some of the things I learned along the way that proved to be beneficial. As you begin to experience this new way of life, keep the following in mind and stay the course:

First, **be patient and trust the process.** Place your focus on the journey, not the end goal. The journey is where transformation takes place. Have faith that what's happening to you along the way will eventually get you to the place you need to be.

Spend some time alone. There's a lot of temptation out there and things designed to keep you distracted from what's real. Dedicate some alone time to think about your life up to this point and where you want it to go from here. Process your emotions, and take a hard, honest look at yourself to see what changes need to be made. Take some time away from those things and just be with yourself.

Accept that challenges will continue to come. Despite the self-care routine you put in place, there will be times when you feel like you are not making much progress towards healing. You may think about what happened to your marriage and get emotional again. This is a natural part of the process, so give yourself some grace. What you are experiencing is what a lot of divorcees experience, including me. It is during these moments that you have to remember that life is designed to challenge you. This is what helps you grow mentally and spiritually.

In order for you to develop new ways of thinking and behaving, the old ways must die. I learned to let go so I could grow through my divorce. My insecurities and fears, my anger and resentment, parts of my ego—they all had to go. They were keeping me stuck in the past. I developed a new attitude to let the past go and be more present focused, which is making for a brighter future. I surrounded myself with positive people and engaged in activities that were beneficial to my overall well-being. I enjoyed the journey of life more, rather than worry about the future. I focused on what I could control and allowed life to unfold the way it was designed from there.

By applying what you've read throughout this book, you'll begin to feel a shift in your attitude and behavior. Your inner glow will start to shine again. Things that used to bother you will have less significance and influence over your life, as they gradually begin to fade away. Focus your time and energy on those things that help move you forward in a positive way holistically. When challenges arise, which they will, when you have an emotional setback, remember that this is part of the journey. It's a cycle in life that must run its course, so take things one day at a time. Your ability to push through it will strengthen your resolve, making you more resilient to bouncing back from whatever life brings your way. As you commit to this journey, give yourself grace when you make mistakes, look forward to healing, and step into a new you.

About the Author

Vance Andrée Taylor is a Certified Professional Coach who specializes in relationships. He is the owner of adVancetogrow Coaching, where he focuses on helping men and women heal from divorce, separation and break-ups, to lead a healthy, balanced, and fulfilling life.

As the co-founder and co-host of the former relationship podcast, "Between Love & Hate," Vance has helped individuals from across the world find hope, inspiration, and motivation to foster stronger, healthier relationships. He was featured on the cover of *Charlotte Magazine* where he shared his story of overcoming adversity during and after divorce, and has been a guest speaker at various workshops and media platforms.

Vance helps to enrich his community through volunteerism. Coaching youth football and teaching financial literacy are just some of the ways he's been able to give back. As a result of his community work, he received a Daily Point of Light award from Points of Light, a nonprofit organization focused on honoring individuals who have helped change the world through volunteerism.

He is a proud father. In his spare time, he enjoys traveling, CrossFit workouts, anything adventurous and cultural, reading and listening to anything that inspires, and spending time with family and friends. You can follow him on Facebook, Instagram, and X (formerly known as Twitter) @advancetogrow.

Acknowledgments

Let me first give honor and thanks to God for being the guiding light in my life.

I would like to thank all the people who I've had insightful conversations with about marriage, divorce, or relationships as a whole over the years. Our discussions exposed me to different perspectives and ways of thinking about love and life, and the connection between the two.

To everyone who participated in my survey, thanks for your candid responses. I know being vulnerable isn't an easy thing to do for a lot of people. Your collective feedback will help other divorcees find their way forward on what can be a dark and bumpy road.

Thanks to my early readers Kisha Kincaid, Monica Warren, Jeffrey McIver, Chatima Johnson, Genna McNeil, and Sadie Marie for your time and thoughtfulness. Your feedback caused me to dig deeper and help make this book even more impactful.

Thanks to my clients who allowed me to share parts of their story, and to my son's mother for being an amazing co-parent over the years. My appreciation goes to my friends and family for their continuous support and encouragement throughout this writing journey. And to my son, Vance, thanks for being an inspiration and key motivator for getting this book written.

To Anita Henderson, my editor and book coach, thanks for giving life and flow to a bunch of random words and thoughts that I put on paper, and helping me to find my voice. This book has been a long time coming. Your guidance, patience, and words of encouragement helped bring it to fruition (not to mention you holding my feet to the fire with deadlines).

Thanks to Candice L. Davis and Karin Crompton, my copy

editors, and Emily Roberts, my cover and layout designer, for their expert and attentive work, which greatly enhanced the flow of the text without detracting from its meaning.

Finally, thanks to my mom for always encouraging me to let my light shine, for loving and nourishing me in a way that inspired growth, and for always being there for me, despite my imperfections. Thanks for your continued guidance from above. I can still hear your voice and feel your presence.